No More Job Interviews!

Self-Employment Strategies for People with Disabilities

Alice Weiss Doyel

Training Resource Network, Inc. ✦ St. Augustine, Florida

◆

I dedicate this book to my father, Martin Bernard Weiss,
who taught me that research and learning were gratifying
lifetime pursuits, and to my mother, Ruth Bearman Weiss,
who showed me the excitement and challenges
of small business management.

First Edition

This publication is sold with the understanding that the publisher is not engaged in
rendering legal, financial, medical, or other such services. If legal advice or other
such expert assistance is required, a competent professional in the appropriate field
should be sought. All brand and product names are trademarks or registered trademarks of their respective companies.

Printed in the United States of America.

Published by Training Resource Network, Inc., PO Box 439, St. Augustine, FL 32085-
0439. You may order direct from the publisher for $29.95 plus $4.00 shipping by
calling 904-823-9800 or visiting our web-site at www.trninc.com.

Library of Congress Cataloging-in-Publication Data
Doyel, Alice Weiss, date.
    No more job interviews! : self-employment strategies for people with disabilities /
Alice Weiss Doyel.
        p. cm.
    Includes bibliographical references and index.
    ISBN 1-883302-36-6
    1. Self-employed handicapped. I. Title.

HD7255.6 .D693 2000
658'.041--dc21   00-023414

Contents

Foreword

I met Alice Doyel in the fall of 1995 at a training event we hosted in Missoula, Montana, that touched on the growing interest in rural economic development and self-employment. As we talked, I realized how complicated our profession had made work. Alice made it simple for me by bringing our conversations back to the basic fact that self-employment was the first form of employment and that "wage" employment, or working for someone else, was a much more complex undertaking. And indeed, self-employment is eloquent in its simplicity; a simple act of exchanging goods and services between producer and customer.

Of course, while small business may be founded on simplicity, complexity enters the picture in the form of government regulation, taxes, payroll, financing, Social Security, rehabilitation systems, market concerns, production, customer service, and a host of other small business concerns. Alice tackles these topics chapter-by-chapter, which allows the book to serve the same function as an early chart book used by the world's explorers. Alice directs the reader in specific directions, illustrates the various hazards and tides, but assures us the journey is relevant, realistic, and filled with opportunity. Alice is also a living example of self-employment success, and she openly shares the joys and frustrations one might encounter as they unleash the unknowable potential, chaos, order, autonomy, and interdependence that come with owning a business.

In any bookstore, one can find numerous volumes on small business development, but very few deal directly with the unique, and yet universal, experiences of individuals with disabilities and self-employment. This is a clear and concise volume that recognizes the growing reliance all Americans have on small business and makes the case that people with disabilities are as qualified as any to take their rightful place in free-market enterprise, regardless of IQ score, mood swings, or ability to walk.

Today, it is estimated that over 20 million people work in home-based businesses in the US, and that the self-employment rate is growing at 20% annually. Over 40% of new jobs are created through enterprises employing between one and five people. As e-commerce expands, the opportunities multiply and market equity becomes possible; who cares or knows if an Internet vendor has a disability?

This is a book that ultimately will undergo many revisions, as did those early charts and maps. While self-employment and the disability field have a long history, for the first time, systems, communities, technology, and self-advocacy are making possible an entirely new approach to self-determination and self-sufficiency.

Alice takes an all-inclusive approach, making certain the reader knows that the marketplace is a tent broad enough to absorb many types of people from all walks of life. She dismisses the predictive validity of traditional vocational evaluation and instead notes that each person needs a variety of supports to succeed. She explains the critical difference between entrepreneurial personality types and folks who simply wish to be self-employed. And she makes it clear that one does not need to be listed among the thirty Dow Industrials to be considered a self-employment success.

Above all, this book represents a starting point in the discussion of making a business and its owner successful; identifying the steps that need to be uniquely addressed by each business start-up; accessing the resources in a particular locality; developing a functional business plan and identifying who can help in that process; planning for benefits, retirement, and taxes; the best business structure for a growing venture and the advantages and disadvantages of each; emerging best practices in small business design and disability; self-employment as a job accommodation; and the potential for e-commerce. Alice's book is practical and based on her experience as a business owner and consultant.

The demand for self-employment has reached a fever pitch. It is the latest "next big thing." I suspect that self-employment rates for individuals with disabilities eventually will reach proportions similar to those citizens without disabilities, and it is energizing to see the exciting potential that self-employment holds. In today's economy, it remains to be seen if self-employment is finally the great equalizer. One thing is for sure, we need maps and charts from people like Alice to show us the way.

CARY GRIFFIN
Director of Training
Rural Institute
University of Montana

Acknowledgments

This book could not have been written without the resources and support I have had from so many people throughout the years. These people come from many areas of my life and from a variety of business, human services, and academic disciplines.

My deepest appreciation goes to Dawn Langton and Dale DiLeo of Training Resource Network, Inc., who had the confidence in my ability to write this book on self-employment for people with disabilities and provided me with the means and support to do it. Their skills and knowledge in publishing have enhanced the book beyond my original goals and expectations.

I gained considerable knowledge from a small but fervent group of professionals who preceded me in pioneering the field of self-employment for people with disabilities. They gave freely of their time to provide me with mentorship, direction, and support. Foremost is Dave Hammis, who has taught, shared, supported, and encouraged me from my initial interest in this field. He and Cary Griffin, working together at the Rural Institute (University of Montana), have provided extensive materials for this book including concepts, methodologies, and case studies in self-employment for persons with severe and developmental disabilities. I wish to thank the many organizations and individuals that work with the Rural Institute, whose efforts are reflected in this book. Other professionals who contributed greatly to the research for this book are Urban Miyares (Disabled Businesspersons Association), Dennis Rizzo, RoseAnne Herzog, Dale Verstegen, Patti Lind, Randy Brown, Nancy Arnold, Elizabeth Van Houtte, and Julia Beems ... all of whom have worked tirelessly to make self-employment a viable employment option for people with disabilities.

I wish to thank the people who have helped me through the years to learn how to become a proficient businessperson. My foremost appreciation goes to Bob Arnold, who has been my CPA, mentor, and friend since the beginning of my first business venture. There are many business associates, friends, and customers who have increased my capabilities as we have worked together. Special thanks to Gay Dysert, Chris and Mark Smith, Dan Holley, Harry Alderman, and Shelley Karp who worked so closely with me to make our mutual customers happy.

A special thank you to the members of my family, who have been the greatest part of my life during all of my business endeavors. Thank you, Kimberly and Melanie, for your patience and support. Melanie, thank you for the summer you spent working for me. Kim, thank you for inspiring me with your photography and creativity. There is no measure great enough to express my appreciation to you, Hoyt, my husband and business partner. You have always encouraged and supported any business endeavor that I have chosen. You are a strong, dedicated, and determined business partner. This book will communicate its message far better due to your caring and diligent critiquing of each chapter.

Introduction

I am sitting in a hospital room, undergoing tests for a twenty-something-
-year-old seemingly undefined central nervous system disorder. This seems
a fitting place to begin writing a book about self-employment for people
with disabilities and the role of human services in this arena. As a business
owner with a disability as well as the consultant to the Colorado Division of
Vocational Rehabilitation for the design phase for their Self-Employment Program for people with disabilities, I have experienced the self-employment
process from both sides. This book explains:

- the reasons that self-employment is an essential employment option
  for people with disabilities
- the method for optimizing the prospects for business success for
  people with disabilities
- the potentially powerful role of human services organizations in this
  process

Many human resources organizations have under-used, and often
misunderstood, self-employment as an employment option for people with
disabilities. Prior the establishment of the Self-Employment Program at
Colorado Division of Vocational Rehabilitation, many Colorado vocational
rehabilitation counselors ignored self-employment entirely.

For those counselors who considered self-employment, it often served
as a last option for persons who could not or would not find conventional
jobs. Most counselors felt ineffective in providing job seekers interested in
self-employment with the tools and assistance that they needed. The
counselors also felt powerless in determining how much money a start-up
business requires and when to stop funneling funds into a business that was
not succeeding.

These reactions and concerns reflect the experience of vocational
rehabilitation counselors around the country, prior to the installation of well-
designed self-employment programs. On the optimistic side, the self-
employment programs started in a number of states are turning around the
self-employment experience for people with disabilities and for their
counselors. These entrepreneurship programs have begun both within the
vocational rehabilitation system and through nonprofit and educational
organizations.

The entrepreneurship programs consider self-employment an option
for persons who seek self-employment as their employment option. To
complete an entrepreneurship program, candidates:

- experience an ongoing self-assessment process throughout the program

1

- reach defined training goals that reflect their individual education needs in small business management and in their specific business
- develop a viable business plan, with support and guidance from a business and/or human services counselor experienced in business planning
- demonstrate that the business venture has the potential for long term success

When the process is carried out in a thorough, professional, and consistent manner, the people and businesses that are likely to succeed will have the support of the human services system. Even those people who participate in a self-employment program, but who choose not to pursue self-employment, still will have an educational and pragmatic experience that will strengthen their understanding of themselves and of their employment goals.

This book addresses the entrepreneurial resources that are available for persons with disabilities and the roles of human services organizations in providing access to these resources. It covers strategies and approaches that optimize success for both the entrepreneurs with disabilities and human services organizations. It also offers case studies of businesses started and owned by people with disabilities that illustrate the application of these concepts.

Case Studies

There are no "typical" business owners with disabilities to provide us with classic or prototypical case studies. Business owners with disabilities are diverse in their socioeconomic and ethnic origins, in the type and severity of their disabilities, and in the vast array of businesses that they create and run. To portray a few case studies as representative of business owners with disabilities in general risks producing misinformation and bias. However, important factors affect business planning for all prospective entrepreneurs with disabilities that these studies illustrate:
- developing concise, straightforward mission statements
- determining company goals and business objectives
- ascertaining the personal goals and objectives that the entrepreneur hopes will result from owning and running the business

These factors answer the questions of "why" the entrepreneur is pursuing a specific business and "what" he or she expects to accomplish. It is only after these factors are established that the prospective entrepreneur can move on to determine "how" to create an effective business by designing plans for marketing, operations, and finance.

Most business owners with disabilities have many potential methods for "how" to manage the business. These methods change in response to customers, economic factors, needs of the business, and personal needs of the business owner. But if the business owner stays focused on "why" he or she created the business and "what" he or she expects from it, the business will have a basis for continuity and longevity. Other employees, consultants, associates, and advisors can provide options for "how" to manage the business, but the owner is the person who must stay focused on "why the business was established" and "what it intends to accomplish."

The first case study provides a sixteen-year perspective of my own businesses. It depicts many of the changes that occurred over time in the business world, in my disabilities, and my family life that both positively and negatively impacted the stability and growth of the businesses. The narrative illustrates both productive and detrimental decisions and actions that I took. It teaches that despite obstacles and errors, businesses owned by persons with disabilities can survive and succeed over time, producing income and increasing the quality of life for the owners.

The next three case studies focus on businesses started and operated by persons with severe disabilities, whose options for satisfying and rewarding conventional employment were extremely limited. They cover designing the business concept, the development of the business, and the business start-up. All three of these entrepreneurs had the advice, assistance, and support of human services professionals.

Finally, the book ends with a short interview with David Hammis, who works extensively with people with severe, developmental, and psychiatric disabilities in their pursuit of self-employment. He is employed by The Rural Institute at the University of Montana, where he is the director of the Montana Consumer Controlled Careers Project.

The Rural Institute focuses considerable effort on self-employment for people with severe and development disabilities. They contributed the first two case studies used here, as well as examples used throughout the book. The third case study is from the Arkansas Support Network, Inc. Although self-employment for people with disabilities has gained increasing acceptance in human services organizations, people with severe disabilities often have been left out of the process. The goal of the Rural Institute is to develop innovative methods for people with severe disabilities to create small businesses that suit both the needs of the individual and the business needs of his or her community.

Their approach has been effective because it starts with an optimistic attitude that people with severe disabilities can be potentially successful candidates for self-employment. A key feature of their approach is to develop new small business creation methods as well as modifying existing methods to fit the needs of people, using person-centered practices.

The methods that succeed for people with severe disabilities are based on good business start-up practices (which would apply to any business), and good person-centered supported employment practices. Supported employment is a relatively new approach to the employment of people with severe disabilities. It provides long-term, ongoing support as needed throughout the term of employment.

Supported self-employment does not utilize human services providers on an ongoing basis to any greater extent than would be used in conventional employment. Supported self-employment human services providers first work with the person to find and develop a viable business concept. As the development of the business progresses, their primary goal focuses on finding and establishing "natural" business, economic, and community support connections. In *Developing Natural Support in the Workplace: A Practitioner's Guide*, Stephen Murphy and Patricia Rogan define these natural supports as any assistance, relationship, or interactions that:

- allow a person to secure, maintain, and advance in a community job of their choosing
- correspond to the typical work routines and social actions of other employees
- enhance individuals' work and non-work social life among their co-workers and other members of the community

Murphy and Rogan include the following examples of natural supports:

- job/task support
- social/emotional support and relationships on and off the job
- personal care assistance
- support with work-related activities (e.g., banking, transportation)
- technological support[1]

Certainly, these parameters apply to self-employment as readily as to conventional employment. The primary difference is that in self-employment, as part of their jobs individuals have some additional management roles that they must perform either on their own, or with the assistance of other employees or outside business service providers. The definition of the job is therefore expanded, and the natural business supports for these expanded functions may be different from, but not in conflict with, those of conventional employment.

Source:

1. Murphy, Stephen and Rogan, Patricia, (1994). *Developing Natural Supports in the Workplace: A Practitioner's Guide*, St. Augustine, FL: Training Resource Network, Inc.

CASE STUDY I
The Life of a Business:
Changing, Growing, Persisting

The majority of this book is dedicated to methods for people with disabilities to successfully start businesses. However, for entrepreneurs with disabilities to achieve the income, job satisfaction, and lifestyle they desire, the businesses must be able to succeed over time. This is a challenge for all businesses, but many business owners with disabilities have additional challenges as their disabilities change over time.

I would like to begin by using my own businesses to portray the types of changes and challenges that can occur to a business owned by a person with disabilities. My businesses were not always a picture of success, but they certainly have provided me many learning experiences. I hope that my experiences, both good and bad, can serve as learning tools for other entrepreneurs with disabilities.

My Background Before Starting My Businesses

After completing an undergraduate degree in business administration in 1966, I worked in market research for a broad range of companies in the US Midwest for nine years.

In 1972, three years before my acquired disability, I married Hoyt Doyel, who is still my husband after twenty-eight years. In 1975 we moved from Chicago to Dallas, where Hoyt had been offered a position as a human resources consultant.

While I was looking for permanent employment for myself, it became apparent that I was not recovering from a persistent virus. In fact it was causing me central nervous system problems. (These problems have had a relapsing-remitting pattern, progressing over time for the last twenty-five years.)

I found that my health was such that I could not work at a full-time job, or even a part-time job on a predictable basis. However, my health did improve to the point where I could enjoy volunteering at a school for children with severe disabilities. I still had the hope that my health would improve to normal or near normal, so I decided to use this period of gradual recovery to obtain an MS in communications disorders. The flexibility of graduate school allowed me to complete my degree, but at graduation time I still was not physically capable of returning to full-time employment.

I continued at the university, working on research projects in acquired language disorders in adults (aphasia) and taking PhD courses in related subjects. The work was interesting and intellectually rewarding, but the stipends for the research were modest.

By 1980 it was clear that permanent, full-time employment was not in my future. However, my health had stabilized for quite a while and I had created a satisfactory life. Hoyt and I decided this was an opportunity to consider expanding our family to include children. We could afford to live on Hoyt's salary, and my health was at a point where I could care for children.

We made the decision to adopt. We felt confident that I was physically able to raise a child as long as raising that child did not require extensive physical exertion on my part, since such exertion caused relapses of the central nervous system problems. We adopted Kimberly Lynn, age nine, in 1981 and Melanie Rose, age six, in 1982. The girls were my primary focus during this time, though I did continue to do limited research with the university, primarily from my home.

During a vacation in the Colorado Rocky Mountains, I had experienced improved health compared to how I fared in Dallas. Consequently, in 1983 Hoyt requested to be moved to his company's Denver office, and the family relocated to a suburb in the foothills of Denver. My health improved with the cooler, drier climate and the higher altitude. 1984 found the girls relatively settled in their new school and community, so I decided to look for part-time work. I was not yet in physical condition to drive into Denver on a regular basis. Without driving into Denver, my job choices were limited and salaries low.

Slowly Starting My First Business

In 1983 Hoyt had bought an IBM personal computer with the intent of using it for working on business projects at home. He never used the computer for this purpose, but suggested that I might learn to use some of the software programs while the girls were in school. Lotus Version 1A had just come out, with a manual that was almost unintelligible to nontechnical users. I spent many hours each week learning Lotus, DOS, and other software programs.

The use of Lotus as a business tool was apparent. However, there were no training books or courses on Lotus for businesspeople. Even the technical support people at Lotus had limited knowledge and would ask you to call them back if you figured out a new method or resolved a problem.

The amount of time necessary for a business owner or employee to learn the software was prohibitive for most small businesses. In contrast, I had the time to learn the software, as well as having the business, math, and basic computer background to succeed. In addition to developing spreadsheets in Lotus, I created automated computer programs with Lotus' limited computer language.

I enjoyed the learning process, which allowed me to work around my health needs and my children's schedules. My main activity during my first year in business was learning about software, computers, and how to effectively use them in small businesses.

I had some luck leading me in this path toward self-employment. One difficulty with learning Lotus and other software at the time, was the cost of long-distance telephone calls to technical support, which often included extensive waiting time. However, Lotus published an otherwise undisclosed toll-free number in *Scientific American* in just one issue. Using this knowledge, I accessed the technical support I needed for unlimited amounts of time without creating an excessive expense.

A more significant happenstance came in early spring, when I created a Lotus spreadsheet for our income taxes for my meeting with our CPA. The CPA was impressed with my computer spreadsheet capabilities. He told me to call him back in May, when he would have some clients who could use my expertise. He was true to his word. Though some situations ended up as a lot of marketing work with no results, he led me to my first substantial customer. The company needed programming in dBASE III, which was just coming to market. I learned to program in dBASE while working for this customer. Now I had the tools to start my business on a serious basis.

The Business Evolves

In the beginning I designed computer spreadsheets and databases, and trained businesspeople to use the spreadsheets that I designed. I created an easy-to-follow Lotus instruction manual with another businesswoman. Some customers eventually wanted training to design their own spreadsheets. Many customers wanted me to support other software products that they had purchased.

Soon I found that it was easier and more profitable to sell people software than to service software sold by another vendor. When I sold a software package, I included installation and basic instruction in the price. Customers were pleased to purchase software that was supported by someone who treated them fairly and understood small business needs and issues.

Most of my customers in the early years had never touched a computer before, whether they were the employee or the business owner. Whether I sold software, consulted, or trained, I let the customers know that they could count on me when they had problems. Knowing that I would be there for them gave them the confidence to grow in their jobs or run their small businesses in a more effective manner.

Combining the sale of products with related and complementary consulting services worked well for the business, since some years there was more demand for software and other years for consulting. This complementary balance of products and services helped to sustain the business through a weak Colorado economy. It was also a positive strategy for my health needs, since software sales and support required less time at my clients' offices than did software training or spreadsheet and database application development.

My business stayed focused on application software, but I created relationships with other small business owners to provide my customers with a full range of computer services. I had business associates who worked with computer hardware and networks, worked with operating systems, were CPAs and public accountants, and provided printed forms and other computer supplies. This complementary support allowed my one-person business to satisfy a wide range of small business computer needs. Working with these business associates increased my knowledge in all aspects of the field. It also proved to be a network that provided emotional and social support.

As more businesspeople learned the basics of general business software, I focused my business on accounting software sales, consulting in regard to accounting software, and designing spreadsheet applications. I offered consulting services to my clients for training, support, and the design of more complex applications for the accounting software. The spreadsheet applications that I developed for clients complemented the accounting software's capabilities.

Some Successful Business Solutions

The greatest challenge for me as a business owner with disabilities was balancing my business needs, my family needs, and my health needs. Most of the challenges were related to time and energy. Often, dealing with these challenges was by trail and error. I handled these problems in a variety of ways in order to succeed.

For example, I was able to keep my start-up costs limited to an IBM personal computer and software that I purchased from my family, other software that I purchased as a dealer at wholesale or demo prices, computer magazines, and basic office supplies. I used a computer and software that was already purchased by my family, which meant that I did not need to try to get a bank loan. I paid my family back for the computer, software, and other supplies as the business made money, rather than on a set payment schedule. This gave me the flexibility to start my business on my own time schedule.

I ran the business from an office in my home. With this location, I could rest, do physical therapy, satisfy other health needs, and usually be home when the girls returned from school. Working from home kept my basic operating costs low. Although there were months when I did not make enough money to pay myself a full salary, I still was able to cover my basic business costs and pay all my vendors on a timely basis.

I controlled my working hours to some degree. Although I did work long hours some weeks, I did not work full-time on a regular basis. I scheduled any family matters that were time sensitive into my "work" calendar in the same manner as client appointments and projects, per Hoyt's suggestion. That small change brought incredible balance to my life. I could then find time to take care of my own health needs. I scheduled most client appointments in the morning, when I had more strength than later in the day. This was easy to do, since I could honestly assure clients that they would be more focused, alert, and learn more before their day got filled with other activities. Consequently, we could both work when we were at our best.

I worked at balancing days at client locations in the city with days at my home office, where I could rest when I needed. The balance was not perfect, but it was exceedingly more effective than working as an employee for someone else's business.

I made time for the extensive learning that was necessary in this field. I extended my knowledge by using client projects as an opportunity to develop new concepts and methods. I did this type of "learning" only with customers with whom I had an excellent rapport. I would not bill the client for my basic learning time, keeping the fees for my services competitive. The client would have patience with my learning time, and in return they would get a little extra work for their money.

I did not require the business to produce enough revenue to support myself independently. Since Hoyt's income was supporting the family, we had made the decision that my self-sufficiency was not necessary as long as the business helped to contribute income to the family and provided work that was satisfying. I took time away from the business for personal, family, and unrelated business matters, which I could not have done if I had needed to be self-supporting.

An Attempted Business Expansion

What happened next will unfortunately illustrate what can happen when a person with disabilities tries to make business decisions without considering the consequences to his or her health. I decided to set up an office space outside of my home. The office was less than a fifteen-minute drive away, allowing me to readily come home when I needed to rest or eat. However, so much of my equipment and work materials were at the office, that I ended up not coming home when I needed.

When my office was at home I usually controlled the food that I ate, which was important to my health. I could have made the right kinds of lunches to take to the new office. However, I ate out at restaurants with friends as a way to get out of the office and to socialize. This had a gradual deteriorating effect on my health.

I shared the new office space with a business associate, who specialized in computer hardware and operating systems. Our complementary abilities appeared to make this a good decision. Although I spent considerable time with this person before agreeing to the office sharing/business arrangement, I did not realize the personal and business conflicts we would have once we shared office space. The arrangement ended up being very stressful and finally untenable. I believe in both formal and informal partnerships, but I learned one must be thorough in evaluating the potential partner before making a decision.

I spent far more hours than I should have assisting my business associate in getting his business up and running, including getting his long neglected bookkeeping up-to-date. I did not get the rest or other self-care that I needed. I have learned that a business owner with disabilities cannot run his or her own business, then assist another business owner, unless that effort is reciprocated equitably.

Although I was the healthiest that I had been in years when I started my hoped-for expansion, in less than a year I was the sickest and most disabled that I had ever been. It took me months to gradually recover; even then I ended up with new disabilities that affected both my business and my personal life. Although I could work only on a limited basis from home for quite a while, the business was a positive factor to me. It made me stretch my mind and body to recover; and the work that I was able to do gave me confidence that I could regain more of my capabilities.

Although my attempt at an expansion failed, I believe that an expansion could have succeeded if I had realistically evaluated strengths and limitations, or I had listened to Hoyt's perceptive evaluation of my health needs. I made mistakes and errors in judgment, too many to overcome. I hope that this will not discourage business owners with disabilities from trying to expand; however, it can provide warnings for some of the potential pitfalls.

Reducing the Work Load

Two new health factors were affecting my ability to do business. I was no longer able to drive due to increased visual perception problems, and I was tiring more easily, making my past working schedule no longer possible.

To resolve these problems, I hired a full-time employee to drive me, work in the office, and do most of the housework. Having the housework taken care of left me with energy to put toward the business. This was costly for a part-time business with limited income, but it allowed the business to continue. Without self-employment, I would not be employable at all.

To further resolve the problem of fatigue, I decided to greatly limit my marketing efforts. I wanted to work less and I had a base of loyal customers, so marketing was no longer as important. I did acquire some new customers through referrals, but I limited marketing to the most likely prospects. Marketing required a lot of energy and time, with a demonstration of the accounting software taking two to three hours. My goal became keeping the business going, although less profitably, with minimal marketing. This strategy also allowed me to have more time at home for both family matters and for my own health.

Life Changes and New Opportunities

The above situation worked comfortably, providing modest income, for well over a year. Then, in the fall of 1991, Hoyt left the company where he was a human resources consultant. The company that had hired him in 1975 had been bought out by a Fortune 500 company.

After several years under the new ownership, Hoyt decided he could not agree with many of their policies. It was time to move on, but there were no promising opportunities in his field in Denver at that time. We either needed to move away from Denver, or we needed to start our own business.

We decided to stay in Denver and start a human resources consultant business, based on Hoyt's successful sixteen-year career in this field. In October 1991 we incorporated Effective Compensation, Inc. (ECI), providing human resource compensation consulting services on a national basis to for-profit businesses, non-profit organizations, and government entities. Unlike my small home business, this was an expensive business to start-up and to run. Although we had money to live on for a significant time, we did not have the luxury of starting and learning slowly. We needed to understand and run the business effectively in a relatively short time.

The experience that I had as an entrepreneur with disabilities had substantial value related to getting us running effectively. I not only had my own small business experience, but the experiences of over 200 customers and of the many accountants with whom I had worked. I had worked with company owners, financial controllers, and bookkeepers for all types of businesses in Denver during a time when the economy was weak. Many small businesses had closed down during that time, but those that had survived understood good business practices. I had learned as much working with my customers as they had learned from me, particularly in the area of financial management.

Now that Hoyt and I were starting a consulting company, I was instrumental in getting the business going from an operational and financial point of view, so that he could focus on the marketing and consulting aspects of the business. This was a business partnership where we knew and respected each other's values, ethics, and work habits. Although business relationships with spouses or life partners can have difficulties and tensions, this business relationship has lasted successfully for nearly a decade.

It turned out that some of our best resources for putting together and maintaining ECI were my business associates from my computer consulting business. ECI became a customer of a family-owned business associate from my consulting business who had supported my customers' computer hardware and operating systems needs. We established a monthly computer support contract with them, which is still in place today. When ECI had grown sufficiently, they installed our computer network. Each time that ECI moved to larger office space, they worked diligently before and after the move to keep our business running as smoothly as possible in the transition. My relationship with the owners of this company has lasted for over a decade.

The family-owned business that provided forms and supplies for my clients became an indispensable vendor to ECI. The owner not only sold us furniture and supplies at good prices, but provided us referrals to many other business resources. She always let us know when we could get better prices buying from the national office supply chains than from her. Our relationship has lasted for fifteen years.

My current CPA had been with me since the second year of my business. He "held my hand" through my years of business development, and was always available for advice and recommendations. We had also shared customers, in which he provided the accounting expertise and I provided the accounting software and computer consulting. He enabled us to readily set up ECI, and to manage it effectively from a financial basis. We talk or see each other at least once a month; however, there are times when I call him several times a week. My relationship with him also spans fifteen years.

These businesspeople are far more than vendors. We consider them an essential part of how we manage, maintain, and grow our businesses. Beyond this, they are kind, caring, fun, and supportive friends.

We started ECI in a modest-sized office with Hoyt and one other full-time employee, while I worked part-time for ECI. I did most of my work from my home office rather than ECI's office. I kept my consulting business going, treating ECI as one of my customers. The economy was in recession at the time, but the company was gradually bringing in customers. We bid on a recurring compensation survey with a national business association and were able to win the bid partly due to my computer database capabilities. Now I would also be doing some billable work for ECI as well as the operations and financial functions.

My Health Changes

Life threw us a curve when I was diagnosed with breast cancer in the spring of 1992, just eight months after ECI had opened its doors. The surgery went well, but we knew that my hypersensitivities to drugs would make the chemotherapy very difficult. We decided that I would continue working for ECI, but that I would close my computer consulting business. However, about half a dozen customers pleaded for me to continue serving them, I finally agreed, with the caveat that I would primarily work from home, and there would be times that my health would prohibit me from working. They all agreed and respected my health needs. These were all customers whom I knew well and with whom I had excellent relationships. Keeping up these relationships, knowing that my business had not totally disappeared, knowing that I was still able to make clients' lives better, and even receiving the checks from clients, were all positive factors at a difficult time in my life. My business produced very little profit, but what it did for my spirit and self-confidence is beyond measure.

During the winter of 1992 and the spring of 1993 we assessed my health and our businesses. On the recommendation of our CPA, and with his assistance, we merged our two companies. This simplified my work, since I now had only one company payroll and one set of accounting books to deal with instead of two. I retained my financial and operations functions with ECI. I continued with some database work on the compensation survey, but we hired a new ECI employee who took over the majority of this project. I continued to work for my small group of clients.

Life Changes for the Better

Life soon changed again, this time in our favor. The recession was ending and ECI's business started growing. As ECI grew, my work for the company expanded and required more time and more skills. Among my new areas of responsibility were the company benefits, which we gradually were able to start providing for ourselves and our employees. I also gradually and selectively started bringing in a few more of my own clients for my computer consulting business.

When my health had been disrupted so by cancer, my full-time employee had to be replaced by a part-time driver. The driver not only took me to business meetings, but took me to chemotherapy and radiation treatments. This situation provided support for me, and freed Hoyt to work for the business. Now that both my health and work load were increasing, I returned to having a full-time employee who assisted with household work as well as driving and office functions. This worked well until the end of 1995, when my employee started having health problems and was able to work only a few hours each week. Sadly, after a time I had to let her go, since I needed significantly more assistance than she could provide. I have never returned to a full-time employee since that time. I have assistance with the housework, and I have hired (with varying degree of success) part-time employees when needed.

Deciding to Close My Business

By the end of 1995, I decided that it was time to close my computer consulting business completely. I was not enjoying the type of work that I was doing now nearly as much as in earlier years of the business. I am also a person who likes change. I had run my business for over ten years, and I felt that I needed to change direction. The hardest part of closing the business was losing contact with the customers whom I had known for such a long time. I did see some of them occasionally. But since most of them were a substantial drive away I saw them only when I was coming into Denver for other reasons. I found an excellent company to serve my customers, which made me feel that I was not deserting them.

I continued to work for ECI, functioning as the company's chief financial officer. My duties included financial operations, payroll, and human resources, as well as working with Hoyt on various strategic and operational decisions. Although ECI had moved into a larger office, now with seven employees, I continued to use my home office almost exclusively. I kept in contact with the main office through telephone, fax, e-mail, and my computer workstation connected to the office computer network via modem. I was able to define my own hours for the most part. Now that ECI was a larger company, I had a consistent salary from the business. This was an ideal work situation for me in many ways. The one downside was that I had far less contact with people than when I consulted to small businesses.

Looking for a New Business Venture

Not too long after I closed my business, the time came to get serious about starting a new business venture. Over the previous few years I had considered some ideas that did not prove to be fruitful. Many things had changed in the decade since I had first become an entrepreneur. In our family's personal life, through the ups and downs of my central nervous system disorder, my health had declined. Our older child had graduated from college and moved out of town, and our younger one was in college. And Hoyt had established his business, which was relatively stable.

In the business world, Colorado's economy was strong. Technology that was just emerging (or had not yet emerged) when I started my business was now a part of everyday business functioning. Small businesses were sprouting up in all areas of the economy. In assessing how to approach finding a new business, I decided to look for books on self-employment for people with disabilities. My search for this type of book opened the door to discovering a new business opportunity.

An exhaustive search for a book on self-employment for people with disabilities showed me that there were no books published on this subject. I started to ponder the idea of writing one. I understand a considerable amount about small business from my education, my work as a consultant to small businesses, and my personal experience as an entrepreneur. I knew that a considerable amount of research would be required, but I have always enjoyed research. Both market research and university research were a significant part of my business career prior to starting my own businesses. Research and learning were an ongoing part of my years of self-employment.

I knew that I would enjoy the pursuit of this information. I felt that I could put together information that would help other people with disabilities succeed because I knew the types of information that I wanted and needed as an entrepreneur with disabilities. I knew that to do thorough research in this field and to have good understanding of the subject could take a few years. But I could do the research around my work at ECI, and I had nobody's schedule to follow but my own. ECI had just been through a period of growth and change, which took a significant amount of my time. Now that the growth was successfully completed, I had time to pursue a new venture.

The Research Phase of the New Venture

I started searching the community, libraries, book stores, and the Internet for information, groups, and individuals who wrote or did work in the area of self-employment for people with disabilities. My best initial resources were in the community and over the Internet. In the community I found a group of people who were just starting a support network for self-employed people with disabilities. This allowed me to meet other business owners with disabilities for the first time and share experiences, ideas, and knowledge.

I met a man, John Houser, who had started doing consulting to entrepreneurs with disabilities. I hired him to help me formulate how I could balance starting a new business while continuing my work with ECI and maintaining my health. Later we became quasi-partners, working both for profit and pro bono in efforts focusing on self-employment for people with disabilities.

Through the Internet, I started to find a small number of professional human services workers around the country who specialized in self-employment for people with disabilities. The National Rehabilitation Association (NRA) had dedicated their 1996 Switzer Seminar Series to self-employment for people with disabilities, and had published a monograph for human services professionals, *"The Entrepreneur with a Disability: Self-Employment as a Vocational Goal."* Now I could find more experienced professionals to contact and with whom I could discuss self-employment for people with disabilities.

Several important points were clear to me in evaluating this new venture:
- No books related to self-employment for people with disabilities were published for the general public, and the NRA monograph was the only published book directed toward human services professionals.
- People with disabilities were looking for information on self-employment.
- There were resources for the information on self-employment for people with disabilities, but they were difficult for either prospective entrepreneurs with disabilities or human services professionals to find.
- I found only one other person who was considering writing a book on self-employment for people with disabilities. The market could easily handle more than one book, particularly since I knew that my book would have a different perspective than that of the other prospective author.

Authoring a book usually is not a profitable venture in terms of dollars, but at this point I was more concerned about effecting a social change than I was about money. After all, I still had my other job at ECI.

My research continued over the next two to three years, interviewing everyone I could find throughout the country who had expertise in self-employment for people with disabilities, purchasing and reading numerous books on small business start-up and growth, collecting file drawers full of related information from the Internet and other sources, and contacting small business consultants and economic development resources in the Denver metropolitan area.

While I was conducting this research, I decided that I wanted people to have free access to some of the information that I was finding and developing. I created a web-site that communicated information on self-employment for people with disabilities (*www.effectivecompensation.com/bold-owners*). It has pages that focus on some of the basic concepts in self-employment for people with disabilities, provides other resources in the field, and presents "white papers" written by professionals in self-employment for people with disabilities from around the country.

Starting the New Venture

Although I kept this new business within ECI rather than starting a new company, I needed a trade name that reflected the emphasis on consulting in the field of self-employment for people with disabilities. I came up with the name BOLD Consulting Group, with BOLD being an acronym for Businesspeople Overcoming Limitations from Disabilities. Hoyt came across a greeting card by *quotablecards* with a Robert Frost quote: "*Freedom lies in being **bold**.*" This was the true message of my new business, and we ordered a quantity of the cards to use for marketing purposes.

During this research period I was introduced to members of management at the Colorado Division of Vocational Rehabilitation (CDVR). The chief financial officer, Gary Angerhofer, was supportive of CDVR instituting a program focusing on self-employment for people with disabilities. I wrote and presented an initial proposal. John Houser joined me in trying to persuade CDVR to accept such a program.

John and I also had begun to do self-employment consulting for individual CDVR clients. About halfway through the extensive proposal process, we redefined our roles. John focused his efforts on consulting to CDVR clients. While I also consulted with CDVR clients on a limited basis, the self-employment program proposal was my primary pursuit. In this way John and I each concentrated our energy where we could be most productive.

I had a part-time employee working for me at this time. She had previously owned and operated a retail business. Although she was hired as a driver and office worker, she played a more important role because of her understanding of small business start-up and management.

There were people in management at CDVR who were resistant to the idea of a self-employment program. It took several months of rewriting the proposal, presentations to staff members, and meetings with management before the proposal was accepted. Finally, with the support of the director, Diana Huerta, the self-employment program proposal was accepted. A Self-Employment Program Task Force would meet for three to four months. It was my role to develop the materials for the task force in order for the task force members to learn about self-

Client Diversity in Small Businesses

Being a small company does not limit the range of customers that can be served. Doyel Computer Consulting, Inc., (DCC), chose to limit its clientele to the small business sector, ranging from two-person "Mom and Pop" home-based businesses to companies with up to 100 employees. DCC primarily served customers in the Denver/Boulder metropolitan area. However, there were customers from rural Nebraska to Pebble Beach Country Club in California. The list below illustrates the diversity of the over 200 businesses that DCC successfully served, functioning as a one-owner business with one part-time or full-time clerical worker-driver-housekeeper, and three business associates in related fields.

Accountants/Bookkeepers	Manufacturer-Computer Carrying Cases
Advertising Media	Manufacturer-Processed Food
Automobile Club	Manufacturer-Software
Certified Public Accountants	Manufacturer's Representatives
Computer Disk Duplication	Market Research Firm
Computer Equipment Sales/Service	Medical Offices/Home Healthcare
Construction General Contractors	Motel
Construction Sub-Contractors	Oil and Gas Exploration
Data Processing Company	Sand & Gravel Processing/Sales
Desktop Publishing and Design	Printing Shops
Distributor Engine Parts	Real Estate Development/Management
Distributor Computer/Office Supplies	Receivables Factor
Distributor/Retail Imprinted Products	Research/Educational Institutions
Distributor/Retail Tools and Supplies	Restaurants/Fast Food
Distributor Pipe and Pipe Fittings	Retail Stores
Distributor School Buses	Service Bureaus
Engineering and Design	Statistical Consultants
Hospice/Healthcare	Training Consultant
Home Owners Association	Travel Agency
Insurance Agencies	Trucking Companies
Foreign Automotive Repair Shop	Water & Sanitation Districts
Magazine Publishers	Water Engineering
Manufacturer-Bricks	

Effective Compensation, Inc., (ECI) with eight professional and clerical employees and over thirty business associates, serves business clients of all sizes throughout the nation. The following is a profile of ECI's clients.

Location:	
Colorado	53%
Eastern/Southern US	21%
Central US	14%
Western US	12%
Ownership:	
Publicly Owned	50%
Privately Held	34%
Governmental	12%
Associations	4%
Size:	
Over 2,000 Employees	24%
500 to 2,000 Employees	25%
Under 500 Employees	51%

employment for people with disabilities. I would also bring to the task force (via telephone or in person) experienced professionals who had developed self-employment programs in other parts of the country. Finally, I would present a prototype Self-Employment Program, then lead the task force in designing a program that would best suit CDVR and its consumers. The task force succeeded in designing a Self-Employment Program for those individual CDVR consumers served who were interested in pursuing self-employment. Within a few months, training sessions had begun and the Self-Employment Program was under way.

Focusing on Writing the Book

By the time the CDVR Self-Employment Program Task Force had finished its work, I had a binder full of notes from interviews, shelves of books, file cabinet drawers of information, notebooks full of presentation materials on concepts and programs for self-employment for people with disabilities, experience consulting to people with disabilities on business development, and experience consulting to a state vocational rehabilitation department on self-employment program development. The money I had made from the work with CDVR had been sufficient to pay for the expenses I incurred doing the research for my book, my part-time employee's salary, and my travel expenses. Now it was time to focus my efforts on writing the book.

For the book to be readily available to people with disabilities and human services professionals, I had to find an effective way to publish, market, and distribute it. While trying to find approaches to accomplish this goal, I took time to do some special projects for ECI and to focus on family and health issues. Time passed without my determining a satisfactory method for getting the book to market. Then the answer came from a totally unexpected direction, and it was a better solution that I could have come up with on my own.

As part of the BOLD Consulting Group web-site, I had included a paper that I had written titled, "*Innovative Programs and Inspired Leadership are Making Entrepreneurship for People with Disabilities a Reality.*" It originally was published in a monograph by the Center for Technical Assistance and Training, a nonprofit organization, to follow up a seminar that John Houser and I had conducted for them. The article caught the attention of the owner of Training Resource Network, Inc., (TRN) a specialty publishing house focusing on books, audio tapes, videos, and other printed materials that promote the full inclusion of persons with disabilities in their communities. The article was published in a TRN, Inc., international newsletter called *Supported Employment InfoLines*, which focuses on the employment of people with disabilities.

Dale DiLeo and Dawn Langton, the owners of TRN, Inc., were interested in publishing a book on self-employment for people with disabilities. Further discussions with TRN, Inc., led to my writing the book that you are now reading. I was fortunate to have a publishing company that supported the concept of self-employment for people with disabilities, providing me with editorial guidance in writing this book. TRN, Inc., markets to both human resource professionals and individuals with disabilities, allowing me to reach my two important markets for the book. Although the book took extensive time and effort to research and to write, I had reached my goal of publishing a book on self-employment for people with disabilities. I learned far more about this subject than I had ever imagined when I had started my research, and I had exciting challenges along the way.

Another Curve Ball from Life

As the book on self-employment neared completion, our family experienced another life change: Hoyt was hospitalized and diagnosed with cancer. Surgery and chemotherapy followed. If this was not enough, our office lease expired and we needed to move to new quarters during this same period of time. The majority of my time was spent with Hoyt, with my work for ECI limited to keeping up with essential financial functions. The other ECI employees worked very diligently to keep the business going as smoothly and profitably as possible in Hoyt's absence. A very special long-term employee rose to the occasion, and beyond. He took charge of organizing and handling both his own and Hoyt's client and management work during this period. His exemplary efforts, hard work, and long hours allowed ECI to retain its stability and effectively serve clients during these difficult months.

Although Hoyt continued to work, he found that he could not work at his previous energy level or his usual (often demanding) time schedule. Hoyt decided to cut back his work hours and job responsibilities extensively. This significant reduction in his schedule allowed Hoyt to take the necessary time off to exercise, improve his diet, reduce his level of stress, and generally improve his health. Since the illness, treatment, and rehabilitation activities diminished Hoyt's marketing and billable client time, we decided to reduce Hoyt's salary during this period. This decision allowed us to keep the company's finances in balance and to keep our commitment to pay employees competitive salaries.

Small Business Employee Benefits

Small businesses can provide significant and extensive benefits for owners and their employees. Setting up the various benefits programs may be a gradual process, as a company grows and becomes financially stable. The following are the current benefits for full-time employees of Effective Compensation, Inc., which is a C corporation.

Medical Insurance:
> In System Benefits: Hospital In/Out Patient is 100%, Emergency Room has $50 co-pay, Office Visits has $10 co-pay. No deductibles. Plan maximum is unlimited.
>
> Out of System Benefits: 70% after $500 individual/$1,000 family deduction, with $2,500 individual $5,000 family Out of Pocket, $1MM maximum.

Long-Term Disability:
> 60% of salary, with maximum of $5,000/month, with 6% cost of living factor, to age 65.

Life Insurance:
> $25,000 Term Insurance.

Accidental Death & Dismemberment:
> $25,000 maximum for death or multiple losses.
>
> 50% for individual loss of hand, foot, or eye.

Prescription Drugs:
> $10 co-payment ($25 for some unusual drugs), with no deductible requirement.

401(k) Savings and Retirement Plan (eligible after one full year of service.):
- 401(k) Employee Deferral up to $10,000 of employee's pay.
- 401(k) Employer Matching Contribution, matching dollar for dollar up to a maximum of 4%. 25% vested for each year of service.
- 401(k) Employer Profit-sharing Contribution at a minimum of 3% annually, with contributions immediately fully vested.

Cafeteria (125) Plans, allowing expenses to be paid with pre-tax dollars:
- Medical Care Reimbursement
- Dependent Care Reimbursement
- Medical Insurance Premium

Flexible Days Off:
> Twenty-one days per year, including vacation days, sick days, holidays, and personal days; increases to twenty-six days in the fifth year of employment. Unused flexible days off can be carried over to the next year for use as sick days only.

Professional Development:
> ECI pays employee's fees for: professional and office skills classes, professional examinations, professional books and other teaching materials, professional meetings, professional memberships, and other appropriate memberships.

In addition to Hoyt's health problems, the office move and new equipment had been expensive as well, so we decided to take out a loan to cover some of the capital expenditures. We have a line of credit that we use seasonally each year, but the company had never taken out a long-term loan once the original start-up financing was paid off. The loan was a reasonable amount relative to our assets and revenue, and we felt comfortable with the decision.

We had known, well before Hoyt's illness, that we needed to restructure ECI so that he could lighten his work load in the future and retire in a few years.

Our hope was to sell the company to employees at a reasonable market price when Hoyt retired. Hoyt's bout with cancer made it clear that we needed to quickly effect changes to guarantee ECI's long-term continuation. ECI has a good staff of professional and support people. Earlier in the year and prior to Hoyt's illness, we had decided to start providing stock ownership as an incentive for employees at the consulting principal level to stay with the business. This also would give them more incentive to purchase the business when Hoyt retired. Our "heroic" employee who kept the business running so well during Hoyt's illness was the first employee to become a minority stockholder in the business.

Now our challenge was to hire two more people of his caliber who could market/sell our services to prospects as well as do consulting work in our field. We had tried hiring people at this level in the past, but we never found the type of person that fit ECI's needs and culture. Now finding such people was a necessity. With more senior level employees in the firm, Hoyt could adjust his work load and schedule to fit his health and lifestyle needs, while keeping ECI going in a successful, forward direction.

The Future for BOLD Consulting Group

With Hoyt and ECI both heading on a more positive course, BOLD Business Consultants became active again. The final chapters of this book were written, and this book was published. Speaking at a national conference on self-employment for people with disabilities, hosted by the Rural Institute (University of Montana), gave me the opportunity to introduce this book and BOLD Consulting Group to a group of human services professionals and people with disabilities interested in self-employment.

Our primary goal is to do consulting for human services and governmental organizations that want to create programs to support self-employment for people with disabilities. Achieving this goal is rewarding for me, for BOLD Consulting Group, for the people with disabilities who desire the opportunity to select self-employment as their means for successful and productive employment, and for the human services organizations that support self-employment for people with disabilities.

Chapter 1

Entrepreneurs with
Disabilities Can Succeed

Self-employment is the preferred career choice for an increasing number of people with disabilities. Some of these potential entrepreneurs come to vocational rehabilitation departments and other human services organizations for:

- resources to accommodate their disabilities
- business training
- technical skills training
- business and personal support services
- financial assistance

Self-employment should meet the broad employment goals for people with disabilities: a salary commensurate with the work, employee benefits, and a career path for future growth. Coupling these factors with appropriate disability accommodations can produce long-term employment and greater self-sufficiency. Clearly, self-employment is not for everyone, non-disabled or disabled. However, it is appropriate for far more people than currently are being considered for it by the human services profession.

To be open to self-employment for people with disabilities, you must be comfortable with the facts in this field, whether you are a human services professional, a person with a disability, or someone providing support for a person with a disability. This book provides factual information that supports an optimistic and active approach to entrepreneurship for people with disabilities.

Myth: Entrepreneurs Are All Strong and Healthy

Open a book on "how to start a business" and one of the first points is typically:

A person must be strong and healthy in order to run a business. He or she must have the endurance to work long and hard for the business to succeed.

Such statements might lead you to believe that no person with a disability should even try to start a business or consider self-employment. How-

21

ever, research firmly contradicts this assumption. A study by Tom Seekins of the Rural Institute (University of Montana) shows that people with a work disability are nearly twice as likely to report being self-employed (14.7% vs. 8%) as people without a work disability. In 1983 the number of people with a work disability who reported being self-employed (520,000) was equivalent to the number of people with work disabilities employed by federal, state, and local governments (533,000).[1] The most astounding fact about these figures is that in 1983, personal computers had just begun to be available to small businesses. Their prices were high, the software was relatively primitive, and accommodations for disabilities were almost nonexistent. Since then, the advances in personal computing have massively expanded the self-employment options for people with disabilities.

In a US government report, *Re-Charting the Course* (1998), the Rural Institute figures are confirmed: In spite of severe obstacles, people with disabilities historically have shown strong interest in entrepreneurship. Information from the 1990 national census shows that people with disabilities have higher rates of self-employment than people without disabilities (12.2% vs. 7.8%).[2] Urban Miyares, founder of the Disabled Businesspersons Association (DBA), quotes Department of Labor figures showing a 20% increase in self-employment by persons with disabilities between 1991 and 1996. DBA, a nonprofit organization assisting people with disabilities with their business enterprises, experienced a 35% increase for that five-year period.[3] There is no doubt that many people with disabilities are continuing to be active in entrepreneurship, finding it a rewarding opportunity for employment.

On the other hand, *Re-Charting the Course* openly acknowledges that government-run vocational rehabilitation programs are slow to follow this avenue of employment. The 1998 report states:

"... self employment and small business opportunities for people with disabilities are often overlooked by government programs and by many people with disabilities as an avenue from the public rolls to self-sufficiency. The Rehabilitation Services Administration (RSA) reports that in 1996 only 2.6% of 225,000 vocational rehabilitation clients with successful closures became self-employed or started a small business. However RSA's own demonstration programs on self-employment have reported self-employment rates between 20 and 30%, substantially above the reported rate of vocational rehabilitation self-employment or small business closures."

If the authors of books on small business creation think that people with disabilities are unlikely to succeed as entrepreneurs, it is not surprising that human services professionals would make the same assumption. Why do the facts contradict these false assumptions? Major reasons include:

- It is still difficult to become employed if you have a disability. Self-employment allows a person with disabilities to avoid having to wait for acceptance by an employer.
- By working at home or in a location of one's own choosing, transportation, often a challenge or limitation to employment, can become controllable.
- Within the financial limits of the business, a person with disabilities can create his or her own accommodations, whether they are equipment-related, flexible work times, defining the job to fit abilities as well as disabilities, or having appropriate assistance and support.
- Along with other life skills, people with disabilities bring the skills that they learned accommodating their lives to live successfully with disabilities. They learned how to use both their own abilities and outside resources to live a meaningful life, and will do the same with their businesses.

It is important to remember that some vocational rehabilitation consumers owned businesses before they became disabled. They do not need to learn how to run their businesses, they need to learn how to make the changes and accommodations necessary to stay in business. *Re-Charting the Course* acknowledges that these entrepreneurs with disabilities are frequently being rebuffed by rehabilitation services along with those people who were not previously self-employed.

Myth: Entrepreneurs Have Specific Characteristics

While there are some specific characteristics and capabilities that are found in many successful entrepreneurs, there is no set formula for predetermining self-employment success by a test or checklist of characteristics and capabilities. The number of types and sizes of businesses is so great, that a single "profile" would not fit all of these settings and situations.

Different personality types can successfully run the same type of business with different approaches and different strengths. One person does not need to bring in all of the attributes of running the business. Partners, employees, and outside resources can, and usually should, provide some of the capabilities in designing and running a successful business.

Many of the capabilities can be learned by a motivated person. Many personality characteristics can change if the person wants success with his or her business. In fact, the opportunity for individualism and innovation can provide the motivation for these personality changes.

The specific type or severity of a person's disabilities is not a limiting factor in offering self-employment as an appropriate employment option. In *Bringing Home the Bacon,* Dave Hammis and Cary Griffin of the Rural Institute portray the successes of entrepreneurs with severe, developmental, and mental health disabilities.[4] These successes take time to develop. They require extensive personal effort by both the entrepreneur and the human services profession and the utilization of tools such as PASS Plans and community resources. These efforts are rewarded by providing a path toward self-sufficiency in situations where conventional employment options are extremely limited or not appropriate for the individual.

Myth: Entrepreneurship Is Risky

Although self-employment has calculated risks, conventional employment is far from being risk-free for people with disabilities, especially those persons with severe developmental or psychiatric disabilities. When a business is developed and set up properly, the risks in self-employment are mostly financial. Often, even these financial risks can be minimized.

In contrast, the risks to an individual in conventional employment are:

- not finding work that is satisfying or suited to the individual
- having golden handcuffs instead of the pride of self-accomplishment
- becoming a slave to a single way of doing your job
- not having a career path or job growth
- not qualifying for company benefits
- not having accommodations that are modified with changes in the individual's disabilities
- not having needed transportation, flexible work time, flexible workplace
- losing the job for reasons unrelated to the individual's capabilities or performance

Positive factors with conventional employment are the security of a regular pay check; possibly, a more stable business structure than is found in start-up self-employment; opportunities for jobs that are not readily created in small businesses started by entrepreneurs with disabilities, particularly those businesses that require access to substantial amounts of investment capital, such as in high technology or the biomedical fields.

The positive factors in self-employment are:

- the ability to create a job that is satisfying and fits one's interest and abilities
- the opportunity to test one's abilities and ideas in the marketplace
- the potential to grow and expand one's skills as well as one's business
- the opportunity for greater financial rewards than are offered for most

conventional employment available to persons with severe disabilities
- the ability to optimize accommodations, workplace, and work hours for the person with disabilities
- more opportunity than conventional employment to make new contacts in the business and social community

Entrepreneurs are often perceived as risk-takers, but that does not mean that they take blind risks or wild gambles. Most successful entrepreneurs take well-thought-out risks, based on knowledge of their business, the market, competition, pricing, cost and availability of supplies, employees, resources, and other pertinent factors. They work at determining what it takes to be successful in their particular industry and for their company.

Many resources are available to acquire this knowledge before expensive or even devastating mistakes are made. Industry trade associations, business mentors, business coaches, potential customers, suppliers, consultants, and chambers of commerce are some of the resources used by successful entrepreneurs.

No entrepreneur is right all of the time, especially when he or she is trying innovative approaches to his or her business. However, risks usually are taken after evaluating options and methods of implementation. Actions can be taken to minimize losses, even if the new approach does not turn out to be successful. Each successful business finds methods that work for itself. No business succeeds on luck alone. Successful businesspeople know this and work toward optimizing the probability for their success.

Business risk can affect people with disabilities in a number of ways. If the business fails, the person can lose self-sufficiency. However, conventional employment has a similar risk. If the business fails after the person has put personal assets into the business, or has substantial debts, this could create a financial loss having long-term effects on his or her life. However, if the business is successful, it will create long-term financial security.

One approach is to take the necessary time to evaluate the business' long-term potential before substantial investments or loans are made. Taking time before start-up, or starting the business gradually, can provide the knowledge necessary to determine if the business is truly sustainable.

Another major risk for a person with disabilities is the possibility that his or her disabilities could be affected adversely by the business, work load, and stress. This aspect should be evaluated as part of the business plan. If the person's health might be impinged upon, the plan should address accommodations that alleviate or lessen this risk. Social and medical support systems should be included in the plan to minimize the possibility of exacerbating the disabilities. If the risk is too great, self-employment may not be the appropriate direction for the person. But when a viable self-employment concept can be created that fits the abilities and needs of a person with severe disabilities, the risks that they will encounter become insignificant in light of the potential benefits.

Myth: Entrepreneurs Are Independent Individuals

An entrepreneur may be a "take charge" person, self-reliant, self-directed, a leader, a person willing to tackle new avenues of endeavor. However, to accomplish the goals of the business, the individual must work with a wide range of people and resources who form the natural supports for his or her business:

- Customers are the focus of the business. The business succeeds by satisfying their needs and desires. Customers are often the source of new business ideas, determining the direction the business will take.
- Financial support comes in the form of loans or capitalization from financial institutions, family, friends, investors, credit card companies, community development programs, or micro-enterprise loan funds.
- Manpower support comes from employees, family members, temporary employment agencies, subcontractor, manufacturers' representatives, and associates in related or complementary businesses.
- For other than home-based businesses, office space must either be rented or purchased and maintained.
- Supplies, raw materials, and salable products come from a wide range of vendors who become an essential, sometimes integral part, of the businesses.
- Journals, seminars, and conferences allow the business owner to keep up with the industry and make/retain business contacts.
- Business trade shows and associations are an essential part of the wholesale and retail industries.
- Professionals such as CPAs, lawyers, and various types of business consultants provide expertise beyond the knowledge of the business owners and employees.
- Communication, computer, and technology suppliers and the related support providers are essential aspects of most businesses. Then there are advertising media, marketing resources, designers, printers, and communications experts.

This list could go on, but the point is that successful businesses are not isolated ventures. Not every small business will use all of these categories, but even a very small business will use a surprisingly large number. Look at the range of invoices paid by a very small business and you will see the variety of business supports required. The successful small businessperson creates a myriad of relationships, some of which will last for the life of the business.

A start-up business can mature into an important part of the community. A business provides products or services, offers job opportunities, uses the products and services of community businesses, and contributes to community tax revenues. Many businesses are active participants in community development and charity efforts. A successful business becomes a natural support for other businesses and individuals within and outside of its community.

Truth: Human Services Can Provide
Access to Entrepreneurial Resources

Human services providers can contribute to self-employment for people with disabilities at a number of levels. A full service self-employment program can provide access to the majority of services needed by a person with disabilities to start his or her business. These services include: business training, business plan development, specific skills training and education, assistance in obtaining financial resources, direct financial assistance (particularly in relation to accommodations for disabilities), professional business coaching, mentorship, and other professional business services.

In addition, a human services agency may provide:

- a portion of the above services either independently or in conjunction with other human services organizations, including the state vocational rehabilitation department
- supported employment training to either the business owner or to other employees with disabilities
- transportation services
- its customary human assistance and support services to help the person live a more independent, consistent, and productive life. The agency personnel can be instrumental in assuring that disability needs do not become overwhelming while the businessperson is developing and running the business.
- help to ensure that the businessperson becomes integrated into the community for the benefit of the business, the community, and the individual
- contact with community development groups to assist the businessperson in finding marketable products or services, finding potential customers, and possibly receiving loans or financial incentive

Self-employment is a collaborative venture with a natural supports system for all entrepreneurs, both non-disabled and disabled. When human services organizations utilize entrepreneurial resources and community connections for the benefit of an entrepreneur with disabilities, they are optimizing the chances of success and self-sufficiency for that person.

Sources:

1. Seekins, Tom, (1996). "Rural Economic Development and Vocational Rehabilitation: Lessons from Analyses of Self-Employment as a Vocational Outcome," *The Entrepreneur with a Disability: Self-Employment as a Vocational Goal*, Washington, DC: National Rehabilitation Association, Switzer Seminar Series.
2. *Re-Charting the Course: First Report of the Presidential Task Force on Employment of Adults with Disabilities,* Executive Order No. 13078, (November 15, 1998). Presidential Task Force on Employment of Adults with Disabilities, www.dol.gov. (200 Constitution Ave. NW, Rm. S2312, Washington, DC 20210, 202-219-6081).
3. Miyares, Urban, (1996). "The Enterprising Disabled: A Ten-Year Perspective," *The Entrepreneur with a Disability: Self-Employment as a Vocational Goal,* Washington, DC: National Rehabilitation Association, Switzer Seminar Series.
4. Hammis, Dave and Griffin, Cary (Eds.), (1999). *Bringing Home the Bacon, Inventive Self-Employment & Supported Employment in Rural America.* Missoula: Rural Institute/University of Montana.

Chapter 2
Who Can Be an Entrepreneur?

Is there an easy way to determine who qualifies as a likely entrepreneur? It would be convenient if specific personality characteristics determined if a person would be a successful entrepreneur. A simple list of questions could ascertain if a person should become a business owner. In fact, there are many such lists. However, there are serious problems with many of these that make them useless, even detrimental. These lists:

- are not tested or validated. There is no proof that they predict the successful outcome of a business venture or the capabilities of its owner.
- are used for "qualifying" people for entry into self-employment programs. When lists are used in this manner, it is assumed that these characteristics cannot be taught through business training or learned while developing the business. However, most of these characteristics can be learned by motivated people wishing to succeed.
- have questions that are related to good health, strength, or endurance. People with disabilities will not have positive responses to most of these types of questions. However, we know that many people with disabilities find ways to overcome disability-related problems and create successful businesses.
- assume that people will answer objectively and honestly. This is problematic when the "test" can disqualify people from self-employment programs that would provide training and perhaps financial resources for starting their business.
- become an easy way to turn people down instead of looking for individual potential and determining training to support success.

Are There Entrepreneurial Characteristics?
Over the years *Entrepreneur Magazine* has had several articles on characteristics of entrepreneurs, allowing us to see how this concept has evolved. A 1993 article advocated a list of forty-six questions to determine if a person has the "right stuff" to succeed as an entrepreneur.[1] However, by 1995 this

approach was summarily dismissed. Bob Brockhaus, one of the most cited entrepreneurial studies experts, was quoted: *"Every time you think you've categorized the typical entrepreneur, someone comes along to prove you wrong."*

The article quotes a University of Washington professor: *"... most successful entrepreneurs possess a variety of attributes, among them persistence, energy, optimism, risk-taking, problem-solving skills, and the ability to overcome obstacles and adversity."*[2] These are more general success-related characteristics than detailed lists of skills or characteristics. Not all entrepreneurs have all of these attributes, particularly before they start training for self-employment or developing their businesses.

In 1997 *Entrepreneur Magazine* reported on a Hagberg Consulting Group study that compared characteristics of over 400 entrepreneurs with executives of top companies. Ten traits showed up that differentiated the entrepreneurs. However, Richard Hagberg pointed out that *"not all of these characteristics are healthy for a company's growth ... Many of the traits that help people succeed at the entrepreneurial stage of a company become problematic in the long run."*[3] If not all entrepreneurial traits are predictors of long-term success, what characteristics should we be looking for in prospective entrepreneurs?

By the fall of 1998, *Entrepreneur Magazine* defined the concept by quoting Chad Simmons, the author of *The Anonymous Entrepreneur - 12 Steps to Build the Entrepreneurial Attitude*. The prospective entrepreneur needs *"energy, drive, the ability to think and act in the long-term, persistence, being goal- and risk-oriented, and being a self-starter... have an attitude that propels [him/her] to succeed, whatever the odds."* Simmons clearly believes that this attitude is teachable for those persons motivated to succeed. *Entrepreneur Magazine* illustrates how the concept of characteristics for entrepreneurial success changed from a very specific, defined model in 1993 to a general one today. This general model is supported by many experts in the field.

- The Wharton Entrepreneurship Program
  "A potential entrepreneur needs commitment, drive, stick-to-itiveness."[4]

- Paul Hawkin's companion book to the PBS series "Growing a Business" stated:
  "To start and grow a business, you have to get down and dirty. I don't mean merely hands-on, but with your whole body, mind, and soul. If a business is to grow you have to own it - the acts, habits, functions, jobs, and grunt labor."[5]

THE BEST METHOD TO DETERMINE WHO IS ACTUALLY CAPABLE OF OPENING A POTENTIALLY SUCCESSFUL BUSINESS IS GIVING PROSPECTIVE ENTREPRENEURS THE CHANCE TO DETERMINE FOR THEMSELVES IF THEY CAN SUCCEED.

- In *Inc. Magazine,* George Gendron, editor-in-chief, proclaimed the first of seven habits of highly effective start-ups as: *"Have a founder who is ready, willing and able to learn on the job during the start-up process."*[6]

This general model means that many people have the potential for entrepreneurial success if they are willing to put in the time, effort, learning, and commitment that it takes to design and run a successful business. This means dealing realistically with the financial prospects for the proposed business. It means having the willingness to research, listen, and learn about the market and prospective business so that projections for success have a firm basis. And it means taking the necessary time to do the planning and preparation correctly before the business starts up as a full-fledged enterprise.

The Way to Determine Who Can Be an Entrepreneur with Disabilities

Although there are many people who would like to start their own business, there must be a system to determine who is actually capable of opening a potentially successful business. The best method is giving prospective entrepreneurs the chance to determine for themselves if they can succeed.

Giving people a chance to succeed does not mean simply putting people into a training program or handing them money. It means teaching them about entrepreneurship in a step-by-step process. Given the proper information, training, and experience, they usually will make their own decision whether they can succeed or not. Since this is a step-by-step procedure, prospective entrepreneurs must put in considerable effort and show significant progress before proceeding through the more advanced steps of the self-employment process or receiving substantial financial benefits.

There is no downside to this procedure. People who learn about self-employment can either take the necessary steps toward entrepreneurship or they can return to conventional employment as a means of self-sufficiency. Either way, they will have learned about both the business world and themselves. If they decide on conventional employment, they will have acquired entrepreneurial skills that are sought today by many employers. Additionally, people who have been given this opportunity, but return to the goal of conventional employment, often have a more positive approach in finding a suitable job.

The procedure starts simply by having an orientation process based on the reality of self-employment. Most people considering self-employment do not have the experience to understand what they are proposing to undertake. Orientation should not be used to scare people off, but to give them a sense of reality about business ownership and the process that is needed to reach that goal. All communication should be both supportive and realistic.

Program steps are discussed further in Chapter 6. It is important to understand at this point that most people will make a good decision whether to proceed with self-employment or not if they are given certain information. This includes knowledgeable support, factual information, and the opportunity to learn. This is required to meet realistic goals in the design and development of their businesses. The goals are set to reflect the progress that is needed for developing a successful business. The goals are not obstacles, but rather rungs on a ladder to successful self-employment. If the prospective entrepreneurs do not want to or cannot find a method to reach the goals, conventional employment is always an option.

Business professionals who specialize in small business start-ups are an integral part of this assessment and training process. They provide the prospective entrepreneurs with:
- a balanced perspective of the pros and cons of starting a business
- balanced support and straightforward feedback
- assistance in setting goals and evaluating progress toward those goals
- business information, business training and coaching, and referrals to further business resources

The business professionals also provide objective feedback and constructive recommendations to the human services professionals who are working with the prospective entrepreneurs.

Supported Employment and Entrepreneurship

There is no classification of disability that precludes self-employment as an employment option. At the Rural Institute, Dave Hammis and Cary Griffin show that people with very severe disabilities, including developmental disabilities, can *"become partners in businesses, sole proprietors, and employees with ownership of vital business resources, through creating paid work and profits from the needs of the business and economic culture in each community. If this can happen, as it has repeatedly in small, remote communities (Plains, Montana: Population 1,200; Red Lodge, Montana: Population 2,300; Alamosa, Colorado: Population 10,000; Sterling, Colorado: Population 5,400), it can happen where you live."*[7]

Do Potential Entrepreneurs Need to Develop Their Own Business Concept?

Urban Miyares, founder of the Disabled Businesspersons Association says that: *"Identifying a business in which an individual can be competitive and profitable is more important than trying to match a venture to past experience, product knowledge, or educational background."*[8] This does not require that the prospective entrepreneurs develop the ideas by themselves. Just as people have professional guidance in finding conventional employment, they can have business consultants assist them in determining a business that can be *competitive and profitable.* As in conventional employment, the business must fit the individual's interest and abilities if the goal is long-term self-sufficiency.

Capabilities and Requirements for Entrepreneurs with Disabilities

The prospective entrepreneurs with disabilities may not have all of the prerequisites for starting a business when they begin a self-employment program. However, they do need to have the initiative, optimism, drive, and determination to learn what they need to develop and run a successful business. Before the business is fully started, the entrepreneurs with disabilities should have the same fundamental capabilities as non-disabled businesspeople in order to succeed on a long-term basis. Even when entrepreneurs with disabilities have assistance with the start-up of their businesses, they will need to compete head-on with non-disabled business owners in order to obtain self-sufficiency.

In addition to having the same fundamental capabilities as non-disabled business owners, entrepreneurs with disabilities need to:

- Develop a business with good market potential, usually offering unique qualities or services.
- Develop a business that suits their interests.
- Understand how to manage the chosen business (or have a key person who does).
- Commit themselves to the business on a long-term basis.
- Do what is necessary to make the business successful.
- Be willing to take calculated risks, including financial ones.
- Develop accommodations for those disabilities that will affect their ability to function as successful businesspeople.

Sources:

1. Raudsepp, Eugene, (January 1993). "Do You Have What It Takes to Succeed as an Entrepreneur?," *Entrepreneur Magazine.*
2. Weinstein, Bob, (August 1995). "Motivation - Success Secrets," *Entrepreneur Magazine.*

3. Chun, Janean, (January 1997). "Type E Personality - What Makes Entrepreneurs Tick," *Entrepreneur Magazine.*
4. *Small Businesses Series,* (October 1996), CNBC.
5. Hawken, Paul, (1988). *The Companion Volume to Growing a Business - The 17-Part PBS Series.* New York: Fireside by Simon and Schuster.
6. Gendron, George, (March 1999). "The Seven Habits of Highly Effective Start-Ups," *Inc. Magazine.*
7. Hammis, Dave and Griffin, Cary, (1999). "Employment for Anyone, Anywhere, Anytime," *Rural Exchange,* Vol. 1, No. 1, Missoula: Rural Institute/University of Montana.
8. Miyares, Urban, "Actions," Bold Business Consultants web-site: www.effectivecompensation.com/bold-owners.

> You read a book from beginning to end. You run a business the opposite way. You start with the end, and then you do everything you must to reach it.
> – HAROLD GENEEN

Chapter 3
Perspectives on Entrepreneurship Training

Entrepreneurship training has progressed markedly in recent years. The improvements in training methods come after several decades of change in small business creation. One of the first milestones in the evolution in small business creations occurred in the late 1970s and early 1980s. The founders of personal computer and software businesses sparked an entrepreneurial revolution. Most of these entrepreneurs started with little money or experience. However, these companies produced numerous new products that sold to an international market that had not previously existed. These entrepreneurs created a revised perspective of small business formation that spread to other sectors of the economy.

Ironically, during this same period low-technology cottage industries emerged when members of the counterculture became part of the economy. They found the world of small business appealing in their search for individuality, self-expression, and independence. Many of these businesses succeeded, with some growing into sizable enterprises.

By the mid-1980s, new personal computer and communication technologies provided tools for small business growth in all areas of the economy. People who never considered opening a business, due to employee and equipment costs, began creating competitive businesses. Many of these enterprises were born in people's homes, moving from part-time endeavors to full-blown businesses.

In the late 1980s and 1990s, many of the giant American corporations had large-scale employee layoffs. The tighter job market and financial insecurity created by these layoffs led many people who formerly would have remained in the corporate sector until retirement to consider self-employment.

During this same time, many Baby Boomers had obtained corporate business experience and financial security. Boomers could afford to start their own businesses or could find the financial resources to do so. With corporations no longer providing security, many Boomers found self-employment no riskier than traditional employment. They saw the chance to have more control over the direction of their careers, and the opportunity to set their own challenges.

The 1990s brought the Internet into millions of homes and businesses throughout the world, offering both the allure and the challenge of e-commerce. By the end of the decade, e-commerce advertisements penetrated all forms of advertising media. However, most businesses still did not have a clear path for effectively marketing of their web-sites. Generally, web-sites supported or supplemented the businesses' primary marketing efforts.

During the 1990s Generation X-ers came of age, having experienced more personal freedom than their parents. These independence-minded Gen X-ers found entrepreneurship suited their lifestyle. By 1998 *The American Enterprise* magazine reported that *"one-fifth of all small business owners in America are Gen X-ers, and the business start-up rate among people age 25 to 34 is three times that of any older age group."*[1]

The 1990s also saw self-employment as a means to self-sufficiency for people with low incomes who had limited employment prospects. Nonprofit organizations became a key force in moving people from welfare programs or low-paying jobs into small business ownership.

The 21st century sees Generation Y-ers providing a new group of potential entrepreneurs. With the majority having working mothers, this group has considerable independence. With 60% having access to home computers by the age of seven, Gen Y-ers technology capabilities will greatly outstrip the Gen X-ers.[2] The factors that fueled the Gen X-ers' drive toward entrepreneurship is magnified in Gen Y.

Impact on Entrepreneurial Opportunities

The consequence of these economic and social changes is that there is a far larger and more diverse group of people becoming entrepreneurs today. This growth and diversity is the driving force in the current changes in entrepreneurial training. Today entrepreneurship is taught to a wider range of people than was previously considered possible. People are taught not only the "how-to's" of small business creation, they are trained to develop entrepreneurial thought-processes, creativity, problem-solving, and communication skills.

Entrepreneurial Training

The objective of entrepreneurial training is to provide the prospective business owners with the business tools, knowledge, and entrepreneurial skills to create successful businesses, providing those owners with long-term employment and self-sufficiency.

To succeed as a business owner requires business knowledge and entrepreneurial skills, whether obtained formally or informally. Some people appear to "innately" have many entrepreneurial capabilities. Others gain them through life and business experience, while other people learn them through more formal educational programs. Business training takes people from where they are in the entrepreneurial learning process and continues their education. Entrepreneurial educational goals include learning:

- hands-on processes for designing, developing and managing the selected business
- creativity, innovation, inventiveness and applying these capabilities
- methods to prevent or minimize problems that could potentially damage the business
- problem-solving techniques for resolving difficult business problems
- strategies to address the ongoing changes and growth of the business
- interpersonal and communication skills, including managerial, marketing, and sales capabilities
- what effect the entrepreneur's disabilities will have on the business, and what accommodations are necessary to put the business on a competitive footing with businesses owned by non-disabled persons

The Wide Range of Methods of Entrepreneurship Training

The educational process can take many paths. A prospective business owner should use several of these methods in order to acquire the education and experience necessary for entrepreneurship. This learning process is particularly important before the business starts up, since most new businesses do not have extensive financial resources to bounce back from significant errors, gambles, or miscalculations. However, the educational process does not end at the start-up of the business. Many of the following learning procedures continue through the development and growth of the business:

- college degree programs in entrepreneurship, whether at the junior college, undergraduate, or graduate level
- programs designed to teach basic entrepreneurship and business plan development, usually lasting several weeks. Many of these classes are provided by government resources such as SCORE or Small Business Development Centers (SBDC), or by nonprofit organizations supporting self-employment for minorities, women, or persons with low income.
- one-on-one or small group training by business professionals knowledgeable in the area of small business start-ups: specialists whose practices focus on starting and growing small businesses, or professionals such as accountants and attorneys, who have small businesses as their primary clients.

- small business research and market research, by the prospective entrepreneur, on his or her proposed line of business. This research includes library and other book research, contacting business associations, interviewing businesspeople who can provide information and perspective on the proposed endeavor, finding competitors and seeing how they run their businesses, finding and contacting potential customers, surveying potential customers, testing the product or service with potential customers, and determining the effectiveness of a business location.
- mentoring from an experienced person in the prospective entrepreneur's field of interest, or a closely related field
- mentoring from an experienced entrepreneur with disabilities, especially one with similar disability challenges
- networking with other small businesspeople to share ideas and experience
- networking with other small businesspeople who have found methods to overcome and accommodate their disabilities
- researching and developing accommodations to overcome limitations imposed by those disabilities that could adversely affect the business
- setting up an internship with a small business to learn entrepreneurship or skills for a particular business

Entrepreneurship training can evolve into, and overlap with, the initial stages of business development:
- developing conceptual or actual products or services for the proposed business
- starting the business with a limited financial investment, with a few initial customers
- creating a "test" enterprise prior to making a larger financial investment and personal commitment

The most important aspect in regard to entrepreneurial education is the involvement and the commitment made by the potential entrepreneur. Most of these learning methods are not expensive; rather, they rely heavily on the efforts and creativity of the potential entrepreneur. This in itself is a good lesson in entrepreneurship: learning how to use creativity, common sense, intelligence, and hard work to reduce financial expense and risk.

These learning processes take time. This is also a valuable lesson in entrepreneurship, since business ownership is time consuming and progress at times is slow. Learning time-management should underlie the educational process. This is particularly important for people with disabilities, since living with disabilities absorbs both time and energy.

Training for E-Commerce and Small Businesses

The Internet and E-commerce are evolving so rapidly that information printed today can be outdated swiftly. However, there are some business principles that apply to e-commerce regardless of change.

There are several aspects of e-commerce that are enticing. Internet web-sites can be less expensive to create than a traditional store or office, so the amount of money needed for business entry can be reduced. For example, web-site location, access, and storage costs can be less than rent for a traditional store or office. The need for furniture, equipment, and inventory may be less costly as well. E-commerce web-sites can be run as a home-based business, which is particularly attractive to prospective entrepreneurs with disabilities.

As payment methods and security over the Internet continue to improve, more people trust the Internet for credit card sales, which makes selling easier. Incredible numbers of people in all parts of the world become new Internet users each day, expanding the e-commerce markets exponentially. E-commerce increases dramatically each year, as measured in the dollar amount of Internet sales.

There are also aspects that make e-commerce challenging for prospective entrepreneurs. Since few businesses can survive on Internet sales alone, the web-site costs should be weighed against other, possibly more effective, uses for the money. Web-sites may end up being more costly than they first appear to be. Identifying all of the costs involved in creating and operating a web-site is crucial for business planning. Sophisticated technical capabilities and effective security are costly.

Finding effective vendors is another essential for e-commerce business planning. In the volatile world of e-commerce, many Internet service companies go out of business, are bought out, or may not keep up with the rapidly changing technology. Determining how to maintain and update the web-site is another challenge. Either this work is done by an outside web-site specialist, or someone within the company must learn and keep up with web-site software and technology.

As with traditional businesses, the greatest challenge is bringing in customers. However, bringing customers to an e-commerce web-site is different in very important ways from bringing customers to a traditional business. With the Internet's ease of entry, an unimaginably large number of business and nonbusiness web-sites abound on the Internet. How does a potential customer, who has never heard about your business, find your e-commerce web-site? The answer, unfortunately, is: "With great difficulty, if at all!"

Can a business overcome this marketing challenge? There are ways, but they can be expensive, particularly if the Internet is the business' primary source of customers and business revenue. First, the business owner should determine what a web-site could do for the company. At the most basic level, the web-site can provide credibility for the business if the site contains enlightening, useful, and accurate information. The web-site principally might serve existing customers, by providing them with additional information, products, and services.

The most difficult goal of the web-site is bringing in new customers. If this is your goal, will the web-site sales supplement more traditional selling methods, or will the web-site sales be the primary source of income for the business?

If the Internet is a supplementary revenue source, the company can market and advertise the web-site to customers and prospects in the same ways the other aspects of the business are marketed. The media and means used for marketing the business in general can include the web address and information about the e-commerce site. Additional e-commerce marketing strategies can be employed as opportunities arise.

When the Internet is the primary source of business, more aggressive means are needed to bring in business. At this time there is no universally effective marketing method, particularly for small businesses without the money for advertising campaigns. The less expensive or even free methods of promoting a web-site often are not effective. These include services that promise that your web-site will be submitted to thousands of search engines, and will guarantee placement within the top 20% of the search results.

You must ask several penetrating questions of these kinds of services:
- In which of the most frequently used search engines will your business be listed?
- How long will it take for your business to be listed?
- Will your business listing be erased after a certain length of time, and what does the web promotion services guarantee really mean?

Alternatively, you can try to have the listings submitted on a regular basis by an employee, or yourself. This can be time consuming, frustrating, and often is not effective. It is more difficult for any one web-site to get selected by a search engine or directory when so many web-site submitting services electronically send web-site information to search engines on an ongoing basis.

This is not to say that bringing in customers to a small business website cannot be done effectively. However, it will not happen without doing market research and market analysis and creating effective market strategies. Each company needs to determine if e-commerce is a viable business option, whether it will be a primary or secondary source of revenue, or if it will serve other business purposes. The business owner needs to understand that it takes time and hard work to build a successful e-commerce business, just as it does a traditional business.

E-Commerce Rules

First, the business owner must understand that the "rules" for e-commerce are not the same as those for traditional business. To do the market research, business planning, and marketing implementation, the business owner needs to understand what works best over the Internet. There is considerable published information on this. Remember, e-commerce is in a state of great flux and considerable growth; rules can and do change abruptly in this arena.

Probably the most important rules are those regarding being a "searchable" web-site. In the traditional business world most people can see the need for a good business location, traffic patterns, parking, etc. However, they often do not understand the parallel concepts in the "virtual" world. One could say "location, location, location" becomes "searchable, searchable, searchable" in the world of e-commerce. Searchability factors such as the "number and quality of web-site links to your site" and "number of web-site hits on your site" replaces traditional business concepts like "customer drive times to a business/shopping location" or "types of surrounding retail stores."

When I worked for a marketing research firm at a retail site location in the mid-1970s, there was a set of factors we analyzed that were consistent over time for a given type and quality of business. The Internet is far from having that kind of consistency and predictability. Reports of the Search Engine Strategies '99 conference were written up in a five-part series by Chris Sherman on About.Com. The experts from this conference discussed the challenges that Internet search engines create for e-commerce web-sites. The first rule they agreed on was, "You can't just build your site and expect people to come. You need to submit your site to search engines and directories, and aggressively promote it in other ways."

There is a distinct difference between search engines and directories. The search engines "spider" (search and examine) all web pages and include them in their indices, based on the text used on the web site's pages. Although they filter out some types of web pages, there is no human intervention or editing. The directories organized by category are edited by people, and are smaller but more selective. They are comparable to telephone Yellow Pages.

While search engines provide a greater number of selections, the directories will be more focused on the subject matter. It is not always obvious to the Internet user who is doing the search if they are using a search engine or a directory. Additionally, there are meta-search engines, which Internet users can use to browse a number of individual search engines and directories in a single search.

The goal of the search engine and directory sites is usually to serve their users rather than the e-commerce businesses. Both search engines and directories are "looking" for sites that are simple and quick to load. Information should be easy to find, within three to five clicks. Search engines look at individual pages, so each page should be easy-to-follow and informative, with well-written text. "Spiders" often check information toward the top of the page, much like a person does when they are reading the material.

The HTML title tag is next in importance. It should be short, attractive, and enticing. Key word meta tags serve as a "magnifying glass for important words on a page." Title tags and key word meta tags are hidden from the reader, but visible to the search engines. Off-the-page factors are also considered, such as the number of links from other sites to your business web-site, and the importance of these linking sites. It is more difficult for small businesses to obtain numerous and important links to their web-sites than it is for a large business, government agency, nonprofit organization, or a university.

There are no consistent industry standards among search engines and directories for selecting web-sites. Indeed, the differences in approaches create the unique value for each search engine and directory. Additionally, each search engine and directory has its own explicit directions for the user to optimally run searches with its engine, which few people bother to follow. These factors combine to create unique sets of web-site results from each engine. There is some overlap, but the diversity of results is quite astounding. Run a search with a meta-search engine such as Dogpile at www.dogpile.com, and see the range of response from the various search engines and directories used in the search.

There are shortcuts to searchability. One method is being part of a larger e-commerce web-site that brings in traffic to your business. This is somewhat comparable to being part of a large, regional shopping mall that brings in customers, who will then shop around for products, or placing your product on consignment in a large retail store.

There is naturally a cost to this process, as there is store rent or consignment fees for traditional retail businesses. But this method can save significant work and cost if the larger e-commerce site can bring in the type of customers who will shop for and purchase your e-commerce products or services.

Another shortcut to searchability is paying for a better display position in the results listing from a search engine. Although this is counter to the concept of "the best interest of the search customer" noted above, it is a practice among some search engines. Some are open about the charges when the search results are listed, but not all of them are. This is a currently allowable, but questionable, practice.

There are also different levels of advertising on the Internet, some of which are geared toward specific markets. If you are on a health page, drug and other health-related advertisements will appear or rotate through. These are clickable ads, and often are interactive. Advertising cost, number of contacts, and sales expectations will determine if and what advertising is suitable. Advertising only gets people to a web-site; it is up to the e-commerce business to create the environment that encourages product and service sales.

There are many other web-site design techniques for a site to become more searchable. Undoubtedly, new methods will be developed in the future. Search engines change their selection criteria as industry practices change, which can be challenging to prospective entrepreneurs considering e-commerce as part of their marketing strategy. For more information regarding search engines, look up the report of the most recent Search Engine Strategies Conference on the Internet and other Internet columns and topics by Chris Sherman on About.Com at websearch.about.com/Internet/websearch.

Twenty-First Century Entrepreneurship Training

The old model for entrepreneurship training assumed that people who became successful entrepreneurs were born with the necessary talent. Or it assumed they learned it in childhood from their business-owner parents or their own experience in newspaper routes, baby-sitting, lawn mowing, or similar youthful business ventures.

Therefore, the training programs and college courses emphasized what you need to do to create and run a business. They included courses on business plan writing and courses on a variety of business functions such as operations, finance, and marketing. However, most of the programs did not include courses teaching creativity, entrepreneurial leadership, communications skills appropriate to small business ownership, or collaborative efforts in business creation ... in other words, how to be entrepreneurial.

Fortunately, the viewpoint of entrepreneurship training and education is changing fast. The first change is in the perception of who is capable of being an entrepreneur and, therefore, who qualifies for an entrepreneurial program. Teresa Amabile of the Harvard Business School says current research shows that *"entrepreneurs ... come in a huge variety of personality types."*[3]

With the incredibly wide range of types of small businesses, this only makes sense. People find the businesses that fit their personality, abilities, and interest. Young people, some still in high school or college, and people in their retirement years now find entrepreneurship a welcome challenge. Women continue to be a growing force in small business formation. Both in third world countries and in welfare-to-work programs, people are becoming entrepreneurs who did not fit into the old entrepreneurial stereotype. Many people with disabilities do not fit this stereotype either; however, they have had a higher rate of self-employment than the general population for many years.

The second change is in the material and methods of running programs. Certainly, business planning and management are still part of a basic program. However, today many creative concepts and classes appear in entrepreneurial programs. Changes are occurring in top-ranked business schools and in entrepreneurial programs run by nonprofit organizations.

Some examples from top-ranked entrepreneurial business school programs follow. These programs are listed because their concepts can be modified and used by government and nonprofit organizations.

◆◆◆

Arthur M. Blank Center for Entrepreneurship at Babson College is ranked first in entrepreneurial graduate business school programs by *US News and World Report*. A long established program, it integrates classroom learning with experience.[4]

In 1993 the Freshman Management Experience course was introduced. The class forms teams, with each team creating a new business. The teams create business plans and receive up to $3,000 in seed capital. For two semesters the teams are guided through launching and managing their businesses, which close at the end of the school year. To date, all students have returned the seed money to the school, and have made a profit.

This type of program is particularly exciting, because the money is turned over each year. If the program is run well, there will be no need for additional seed capital funding. Businesses started during the class would not need to stop at the end of the program, but could continue as an ongoing business. Profits beyond the seed money could go into the ongoing business or new businesses to be started by the students, or could be returned to the program to provide additional seed money.

◆◆◆

Stanford Graduate School of Business started its Center for Entrepreneurial Studies in 1997. In 1999, 90% of the MBA students took at least one entrepreneurial course. In 1998, the students sponsored a day-long entrepreneurship conference, with a variety of speakers, including Jeff Bezos, founder of Amazon.com.[5]

Entrepreneurial conferences do not need to be expensive. You can get support from local or state entrepreneurs who can offer insight, creativity, and exuberance for prospective entrepreneurs. Most businesspeople who have started and succeeded in their own businesses are glad to share their experience and knowledge with others interested in starting a business.

Stanford's entrepreneurship program includes a course taught jointly with the School of Engineering. During the two-semester course, teams of engineering and business students conduct market surveys in an instructor-defined market, design a product that suits the market, manufacture the product using the engineering lab, and compete with other teams for simulated sales and marketing.

This teaching paradigm does not require Silicon Valley technology. The primary concept is bringing together prospective business owners with people who can design and create. The same concept could be used if the design people were jewelers, chefs, or software designers. The design people could be students, professionals, or business owners. If the products are marketable, a new business could emerge.

◆◆◆

The *University of Chicago* formalized its Entrepreneurial Program in 1997, offering educational and networking opportunities for students and entrepreneurial alumni, as well as collaborations with local industry and investors. The program is designed to utilize students "enthusiasm, skills, and knowledge."

With joint funding from the Kauffman Center for Entrepreneurial Leadership, the University of Chicago has subsidized paid entrepreneurial summer internships (after the first year in graduate school) with businesses less than five years old, working primarily with the owners or principals. The businesses pay 50% or more of the intern's salary. The business benefits, since the student functions as a consultant to the company.[6]

Developing internships in local businesses is productive for all concerned, if the intern can see all aspects of the business through the owner's perspective and, as Paul Hawkin said (see page 12), *"get down and dirty ... with your whole body, mind, and soul."* The additional benefit of grants or subsidies allows the intern to earn money during this period, without creating a heavy financial burden on the business. Since the business pays part of the salary, the owner is likely to take the intern seriously and use him or her effectively as an employee.

◆◆◆

The Leo V. Ryan Center for Creativity and Innovation at DePaul University (Chicago, Illinois) opened in 1997 to provide *"hands-on learning for creative discovery and business innovation."* The center is available not just to students, but to the business and nonprofit community. Students develop idea generation and implementation skills, as well as innovative problem-solving techniques. The university faculty is supplemented by creativity consultants.[7] Lisa Gundry, director of the center, wants students to find a connection between art and business. She says, *"inspiration surrounds the person who knows how to look for it ... creativity can be taking something that already exists and looking at it in an entirely different way."*[8]

Even in communities where there are no business creativity consultants or creative arts programs, there probably are nonprofit organizations for the arts, human services providers with therapeutic art programs, and business and economic development organizations. These combined resources could develop programs focusing on creative processes that enhance business innovation and problem-solving.

◆◆◆

Harvard Business School (HBS) has offered entrepreneurial courses since 1946. In recent years it has focused on "how" entrepreneurship is accomplished, not just on "who" entrepreneurs are or "what" they do. HBS believes that *"both formal education and informal mentoring lead to understanding the success and failure of others, which in turn leads to skill development."*[9] Simply stated: You can learn entrepreneurship; it requires time and a variety of methods.

The HBS Entrepreneurship, Creativity, and Organization class is designed for prospective entrepreneurs to foster effective, innovative work in the people they lead; and preserve their own creativity. Creativity is the production of novel, useful ideas in any endeavor. Innovation is the successful implementation of those ideas.

The approach is to start with programs that engender creativity in any form, so that prospective entrepreneurs begin to think in this mode. This includes museum tours, nature trips, creative writing, acting, or graphic arts. These activities can be done by individuals or groups. Once creativity becomes a way of thinking, it can be carried over to business concepts and challenges.

HBS also works to bring entrepreneurship and human services together in the Entrepreneurship in the Social Sector class. *"Societies are searching for innovative and efficient ways to provide socially important goods in health, education, social services, environment, and community development. Old approaches seem to be falling short, and traditional government and nonprofit service providers are encountering serious financial pressures. This course explores opportunities for social entrepreneurship via nonprofit, for-profit, and hybrid social purpose organizations, with a particular emphasis on the benefits and limits of adapting business practices to the distinctive operating environments of the social sector."*

◆◆◆

Universities and their affiliates are teaching entrepreneurship to people involved with human services organizations. Cary Griffin of the *Rural Institute (The University of Montana)* developed a training course called Civic Entrepreneurship. Civic entrepreneurship involves the social sector (rehabilitation and other human services organizations) bringing together the public (governmental) and the private (business) sectors to address community issues. Griffin creates training programs that reach and bring together people with disabilities, local government and economic development entities, the local business community, and nonprofit organizations in both rural and urban areas.

He explains, *"Whereas these sectors have often worked at arm's length, the growing global economy dictates partnerships and networks of diverse populations solve critical problems and leverage the wealth of the community. World class economies require world class communities that form economic alliances that benefit all sectors. Working in isolation is no longer an option as strategic alliances become the best method for solving complex problems such as unemployment, isolation, or bigotry. Economic and social alliances seek to raise the standard of living for all community members and the social sector represents a key catalyst in this amalgamation of skills, needs, and resources."*[10]

Government and nonprofit organizations, who work collaboratively with business and economic development groups and local businesses, can learn for-profit business practices and apply them, where appropriate, to their own organizations. Working with entrepreneurs with disabilities offers the opportunity to bring these diverse organizations together for greater mutual understanding and growth as well as entrepreneurial knowledge.

Reaching the Objective of Entrepreneurship Training

This chapter began by defining the role of "entrepreneurship training" as providing potential entrepreneurs with the business tools, knowledge, and personal skills they need to create successful businesses, ultimately leading to personal self-sufficiency. It is clear that entrepreneurship training is not focused solely on designing and running the proposed business. For the training to be successful for a wide range of prospective business owners, it also must focus on developing personal entrepreneurial characteristics and capabilities in the people who will create and run the small business enterprises.

Sources:
1. Ericson, Edward E. Jr., (January/February 1998). "Gen X Is OK, Part I," *The American Enterprise.*
2. Beck, Melinda, (February 3, 1997). "The Next Big Population Bulge: Generation Y shows Its Might," *Wall Street Journal.*
3. Reagan, Brad, (June 14, 1999). "'I Did It My Way' 101," *Wall Street Journal.*
4. Arthur M. Blank Center for Entrepreneurship at Babson College web-site: www.babson.edu/entrep.
5. Stanford GSB: MBA Program: Entrepreneurship web-site: www.gsb.stanford.edu/academics/programs/mba/entrepreneurship.html.
6. University of Chicago Graduate School of Business Entrepreneurship Program web-site: gsbwww.uchicago.edu/research/entrep.
7. Leo V. Ryan Center for Creativity and Innovation at DePaul University (Chicago, Illinois) web-site: www.depaul.edu/~lgundry/rcci.
8. Reagan, Brad, (June 14, 1999). "'I Did It My Way' 101," *Wall Street Journal.*
9. Harvard University's Harvard Business School web-site: www.hbs.edu.
10. Weiss-Doyel, Alice, (August 1999). "Self-Employment as a Career Choice for People with Disabilities," *Bringing Home the Bacon, Inventive Self-Employment & Supported Employment in Rural America.* Missoula: Rural Institute/University of Montana.

CASE STUDY II
Poooh's Artistry:
Business Plan Summary

Poooh's Artistry will produce and market products developed from Beth A. Dean's fine art oil paintings and prints depicting God's beautiful scenery. The primary products will be high quality greeting cards with Christian and fine art themes, from reductions of prints and original oil paintings, for wholesale, retail, and consignment product sales in targeted Christian and general markets. Additional products will include Beth's original oil paintings and product lines of limited edition prints, calendars, and bookmarks.

Founded by Whom, and Why

I, Beth A. Dean, am the founder and sole owner of Poooh's Artistry. I started Poooh's Artistry about eleven months ago out of my home. Since then my cards have been placed for retail and consignment sales with three businesses and I have orders from four more businesses. I've always enjoyed viewing and painting God's beautiful scenery. In the last year I've decided to get my paintings and life's work out to the public to see if others would enjoy the sights as well as I do.

Form and Ownership

This business is a sole proprietorship owned 100% by Beth A. Dean. I am anticipating a natural expansion of my business in the future, and am open to considering general or limited partnerships, limited liability companies, S corporations, or corporate forms of business. Two companies are backing my talents and efforts and may prove to be long-term business relationships that could enhance or alter the current form of my business. For the next few years as I work to become firmly established in my target markets, I expect to retain my current sole proprietorship form of business.

Mission Statement, Business Goals

The mission of Poooh's Artistry is to bring the gifts of nature through quality and affordable art, as a sharing of Beth A. Dean's artistic interpretations of God's scenic beauty, to the Christian and general art customers of the world. Art has a personal meaning to each individual and can express many feelings to the public eye. Until recently, quality art has been bought and sold mainly to the higher financial class of people. Then prints started to be marketed to a different class of people, but still not reaching all financial classes of the public.

Now with technology, color laser prints on card paper equate to much smaller and affordable high quality prints that can serve more than a print you can frame for yourself, but as a gift, an expression of feelings for a holiday or situation that is hard for some to touch with pages of words, while also reaching the most discriminating art collectors as well as card collectors.

I feel my business will do well for many reasons. Every artist touches on a different viewpoint or feeling in people as well as using different techniques and styles. The two product styles of interest, cards and paintings, will go very far as it has been done by other artists. It has also grown at a fast rate. The trend for art on cards is growing nationwide. I also believe the marketing mix of Christian and general card and painting sales adds a unique and yet diverse approach that blends with the core of my life and beliefs and holds the potential to reach tremendous markets throughout the world.

My personal commitment and life experience has led me to this point in my life where I possess the talents and motivations to succeed. I am thirty-nine years of age. I have a daughter whom I have homeschooled and who has completed high school with a 4.0 grade average.

I have been on SSI for ten years. I was diagnosed with diabetes at about age seven to nine. It was not clear to doctors due to many other medical situations. It has progressed over the years. I am a kidney transplant recipient and have had it for three plus years. I have been blind in my left eye for two years. My right eye is also affected by a medical situation. Throughout my life I have faced many challenges and have many friends and personal and professional supports. I have my loving family that encourages and stands with me, including my stepfather who has a business degree as well as a stepmother who is a retired accountant. My birth parents are highly educated in the business world as well and they have all been very supportive. I am excited about this business, which reflects my strengths and talents, and I will succeed.

First year goals: Since I have been in business for eleven months, my first year goals are almost complete. I have prepared and created eight canvases of work; successfully developed card reproductions of my work; printed various small test quantities of cards and sold cards to local and regional retailers; placed market sample cards on consignment; developed a competitive pricing strategy; received my first shipment of 16,000 cards and begun receiving and filling orders; established a variety of local, regional, and national retailer relationships and markets and a simple start-up distribution method; applied for assistance related to my business and disability from Montana Vocational Rehabilitation and the Rural Institute on Disabilities; and I am now poised for expanding my business and increasing my sales.

Third year goals: I expect to develop forty-eight canvases by my third year in business. I will need to expand my current work space, which is partially underway as my daughter has moved out and I now have the potential to use her room for an expanded studio with some modifications. With the addition of an outside staircase to reach my three-quarter story attic, I will be able to store my works and products. I will own a computer soon, and clearly will require my own personal computer training to be complete by year three. By year three I will have established product market shares in the New England states, southern states, and western states. I expect to be firmly established in Montana, Utah, Oregon, and

Wyoming by year three. I will have a solid production and marketing line of products for sale with cards, oils, prints, calendars, and bookmarks. I also expect to have a small percentage of international marketing procedures operating via the Internet at that time. I will be economically stable in my business with a predictable growth pattern to work from for future years.

Fifth year goals: By my fifth year I expect to have developed at least eighty canvases. There will be a planned reinvestment of a portion of earnings into the development and construction of a large working studio and pre-production facility that will offer the opportunity to increase the production of my expanding product lines, with firm international markets in place. I will be employing at least two full-time marketing personnel and several production workers for my expanded marketing and production needs and have a fully integrated pre-production process and equipment in place with contracts with major printing contractors for high volume runs of my products. I will have just-in-time computer ordering and distribution chains in place with major retail chains.

Key Officers, Management

I will be the key officer. I will be in charge of the artwork, design, pre-production methods for reductions and computer scanning, materials used, marketing, pricing, sales, billing, and overall management during my start-up years. I have been an artist for many years. I will bring to this business my creative skills as well as my knowledge of the art world and Christian markets. I also bring my love and passion for art, which will be crucial in the success of this business. I will primarily be responsible for all marketing, but have the pro bono support of a couple in Georgia who are showing my work in businesses in the southern states. They are prepared to financially back me when they are able to obtain orders from businesses in their area.

I also have, through my mother, a contact with a man in Massachusetts, who owns a very large, well-known printing business with a fine artist on his staff. He has given me a donation runoff of 1,000 prints each of scripture and non-scripture (16,000 total) to help get my business on its feet.

Although these businesspeople are not official officers in my business, all have shown a strong interest and are clearly advising me and more, as my business develops. Their combined knowledge totals over fifty years of experience in marketing and printing.

I also plan in the near future to hire someone to help in keeping the paperwork part of the business up and to help in the printing, packaging, and mailings. The woman I have in mind is a licensed teacher with a degree in math and French studies. She has been a personal care attendant for me for twelve years and has been with me since before I started this business.

Markets/Customers Served

The cards, calendars, and bookmarks will be marketed to local, regional (western, southern, and New England states) Christian stores and gift shops. The artwork also will be shown at local art galleries located in Missoula, Spokane,

Seattle, Salt Lake City, and numerous small towns and galleries located throughout the western region. The customers I intend to serve are the Christian-card-buying customers and the average card-buying customer. I believe the marketing mix of Christian and general card and painting sales adds a unique and yet diverse approach that blends with the core of my life and beliefs and holds the potential to reach tremendous markets throughout the world. The cards are in fact actual prints from originals that I do. I believe in the near future I also will be reaching the card collector industry.

I intend to market in the surrounding states and eastern and southern states that I have contacts in and hope to grow nationwide. I started with a small but successful gift shop in Plains, Montana, six miles from my home. I now have products in three other towns in Montana, Idaho, and Spokane, Washington. I also set up at a trade fair in Plains and received good exposure as well as distributing approximately 200 business cards. People are calling me and placing orders from seeing my cards at other businesses in Montana and Washington.

Distribution of Products/Services

My main distribution chain at the moment focuses on receiving orders from retailers, processing them in Montana, shipping from Montana, and restocking large supply quantities from the New England area. I have a few situations set up on consignment, using the same method, but am expecting to stay with the cash-order first approach. I have a major printing shop in Massachusetts ready to begin production runs after my initial stock of 16,000 cards supports enough of a cash flow and reserve to begin placing high volume future orders. From that print shop large orders could be shipped directly to larger customers. In the interim I am processing and filling all orders from my business location in Montana through standard ground transportation methods with some air freight. The networks I have in place cover three national regions.

Industry Profile/Competitive Analysis

The art world is exploding in growth, especially in the northwest and southwest regions of the US. The Christian art market offers a clear differentiation and open market. Hand-painted, high quality artwork available at affordable prices, combined with Christian market profiles, is a market dominated by only a few large Christian printing companies. It is very susceptible to local and regional competition and market share penetration due to the lack of strong sales forces and other unique market factors. I have already received suggestions about licensing my work to one large company, providing volume discounts vs. taking a competitive stance in the less "hospitable" markets. Currently the industry is welcoming me with open arms.

Marketing Strategy/Market Share

1. Traditional Method: I will preview samples of products with owners of Christian book stores, gift shops, tourist shops, and novelty shops by scheduling appointments with owners and then presenting cards and artwork within the

confines of each business. Sample cards will be left for initial sales trials, and orders placed for immediate card purchases and stocking.

2. Utilization of Computerized Technology: This will be comprised of direct scanning or taking photographs of my cards, product lines, and artwork, which will then be converted into an electronic computer file format. The photographic file will then be enhanced to delete any imperfections in developing. Addition of graphical marketing elements will also be added at this phase. The artwork will be assembled into a Power-Point slide presentation. The presentation will be previewed by Christian book store, gift shop, tourist shop, and novelty shop owners at scheduled industry fairs throughout the regions I will be operating in. The computerized file format of the entire presentation would be made available for shop owners to keep on a computer.

3. E-Mailed Presentations: The above computerized presentation would be available for e-mail transmissions to interested regional, national, and international store owners and galleries who would be interested in showcasing Poooh's Artistry's artwork. Interested parties would be prospected via postings within related newsgroups (Usenet) on the Internet. Similarly these same file formats will be available for electronic transfer to referred interested private parties.

4. Establishing an Internet Web-Site: Selected pieces of artwork along with their media and dimension descriptions and prices of each individual painting, card, and calendar, will be displayed for sale on the World Wide Web. The site will be accompanied by a biography describing my background and history.

5. Donation of Artwork: There also will be donations of selected pieces of artwork to charitable organizations, community events, awards ceremonies, hospitals, children's support groups, etc., to aid in fundraising and for purposes of additional exposure.

6. Regional Marketing Support: Another avenue will be pursued for regional marketing on-site at distances that prohibit my travel but can be accomplished from the support I already have generated in Georgia and New England. This method consists of advance mailing of all the above materials to the regional marketing representatives, who will be selling the products.

Personal Reflections on Small Business Development

Business Challenges and Successes: Designing, printing, and distributing the cards and related items is a complex business. It requires many skills, which take considerable time to develop.

The computer technology alone took two to three years to master. Learning this technology enabled me to do printing at my in-home production office, utilizing custom-built computer hardware and specialized software. There is a learning curve in understanding which equipment works best. For example, I found that using a digital camera to take pictures of my art work proved a more efficient and higher quality method of bringing the art work into the computer than using scanning equipment. Doing the printing myself is important, since my orders are still too small to be done with time and cost efficiencies by a major printing company. I am currently learning how to transfer pictures of my artwork and products to CDs, so that I can provide customers and prospects with a visual display of the entire line of products.

Things that appear to be simple can be quite complex. An example is finding the right type of paper at a reasonable price. Different products require different paper stock. The paper stock for note paper is a different quality and costs less than the paper used for greeting cards. Additionally, if the printing is done by different printing companies, each company has equipment that can require a specific type of paper, which can differ from what another printer requires.

Getting a bulk mailing permit was not cost effective for the modest size of my mass mailings. However, paying the full postage was expensive. I solved the problem when I found a printer who would do the mailings for me using the printer's bulk mailing permit. Then the printer provided an additional service at no charge; he did the research to find the appropriate mailing lists for my business.

I am fortunate to have Sunny Alteneder as my personal care attendant. She is also a math teacher. Sunny assists me in a variety of ways in the business. During a time when my vision made it impossible to tell where I needed to paint on a canvas, she would guide me to the right place on the canvas. Then I could continue the creation of my art work. When I have difficulty determining the precise dimensions of the art work on my computer screen, Sunny's math capabilities are applied to produce the exact size for printing.

My greatest remaining business challenge is reaching a broader market, including finding distributors who will effectively place my products in retail locations. I have a dozen retail store customers who sell my products on a continuing basis. At times I give them pricing breaks or offer them sales promotions. My sister in Georgia is working on selling my products to retail stores and also to companies who can use personalized calendars and cards as sales promotion items. I am investigating ways to get my cards into a catalogue from a major company. I also would like to see my web-site be an effective part of my sales effort, and am looking into ways to advertise and promote the web-site. I realize that just being out on the Internet does not bring in business; there needs to be active marketing of the site.

Learning how to run the business: My parents, stepparents, sister, and brother-in-law have supported me and have given me business advice from their own business experience. The printer from Massachusetts, who is discussed in the business plan, is a family friend who has been a mentor to me. My family always gave me support in this endeavor. It was my father's desire that I do something with my art since I was a child. My daughter convinced me that I should use my artwork for a business, and gave me self-confidence to sell my work to the public.

I am now taking business courses at a nearby college, which provides me with the added benefit of receiving free business consulting assistance. My business counselor is focusing on assisting with the marketing challenge of obtaining wider distribution of the Poooh's Artistry products.

Material for this case study has been taken from the Poooh's Artistry business plan and an interview with Dean. The business plan material has been edited to fit the format of this book; consequently, it does not contain all of the information that was written into the original business plan. Most notably, financial planning and projects are not included here.

Dean had assistance in her business planning and development from Dave Hammis of the Rural Institute, her business plan was reviewed by the Montana Community Development Center (MCDC), and she received accounting help from the MCDC and a certified public accountant. For more information: Poooh's Artistry, PO Box 154, Paradise, Montana 59856; 406-826-459; www.pooohsartistry.com.

Chapter 4
Challenges for Entrepreneurs with Disabilities

Roadblocks are impediments that can stop a business venture from succeeding, or even starting up, while challenges are obstacles that can be overcome. This chapter presents some of the potential challenges for people with disabilities who wish to be entrepreneurs.

The goal is to be aware of the potential obstacles, evaluate how they might affect an entrepreneur with disabilities and the proposed business, and then determine ways to work around the obstacles ... or ways to greatly diminish their effect on the business. The result is that the prospective business owner finds positive methods and resources to increase the prospects of the business succeeding on a long-term basis.

Approaching Entrepreneurship: Evaluating the Entrepreneurial Challenges from Disabilities

Entrepreneurial training and business planning for people with disabilities is primarily the same as that for non-disabled people, since the businesses owned by non-disabled people and those owned by people with disabilities compete in the same arena. Some elements of business ownership and management that are pertinent to small business owners in general require special consideration for entrepreneurs with disabilities. Other elements are unique to people with disabilities.

Not all disability-related challenges are apparent before the business starts up, or even after it has been up and running for some time. Often the challenges emerge as unanticipated problems, disrupting the flow of the business and limiting its operation.

In many ways problems derived from business owners' disabilities can be dealt with in the same manner as other business problems. When the business owners determine which disability-related problems might occur and prepare alternative methods for running their businesses ahead of time:

CHALLENGES SHOULD NOT BE SEEN AS STUMBLING BLOCK TO SELF-EMPLOYMENT. RATHER, CHALLENGES SHOULD BE ANALYZED IN REGARD TO THE LIMITATIONS THAT THEY COULD IMPOSED ON THE BUSINESS, WITH THE PERSPECTIVE OF FINDING METHODS TO OVERCOME THE LIMITATIONS.

- either the problems will be prevented or diminished before they occur or
- there will be potential solutions ready ahead of time if the problems do occur, eliminating or lessening the adverse effects on the business

This book addresses challenges of self-employment that are relevant to entrepreneurs with disabilities. Further chapters discuss challenges in the context of business planning and small business development. This chapter and Chapter 5, however, provide an overview of issues that should be considered while determining if self-employment is a viable employment option and during the beginning stages of creating a business concept and business plan.

These issues may not be resolved during these early stages of self-employment evaluation, idea development, or business planning. However, considering the challenges at this point in the process increases the likelihood of clearly understanding their effects on the business, and integrating positive solutions into the business plan.

If some challenges cannot be overcome and create limitations to the business, the question then is: Can the business still provide the potential entrepreneur with the level of income needed to improve the quality of his or her life?

Ways Self-Employment Improves Quality of Life: Economic Stability

For many people with disabilities, a key issue is to achieve economic stability. However, self-employment should not be taken off the table if the business alone does not bring in enough income to achieve this goal. The business should be able to make a profit once it has achieved maturity, otherwise it is an avocation or hobby. But it does not need to be the sole source of income for the business owner. It is very common for non-disabled business owners to have alternative sources of income. This is particularly true during the early years of the business. The person with disabilities may:

- receive SSI, SSDI, Medicare, Medicaid, or other federal and state government benefits
- have savings, investments, trust funds, disability insurance payments, or insurance settlement money

- have income from conventional employment or from ownership in another business, though these sources are less likely for people with disabilities than for the general population
- live with an employed spouse or life partner, child(ren), parents, or house/apartment mates
- receive support from family members, alimony payments, or child support
- receive assistance for their disabilities and daily living from nonprofit organizations

These resources, and other sources of income, all can be included to achieve a desired income level. Ideally, a person eventually will be able to live without government supports. If this ideal is not reached, but this person's quality of life is improved beyond the minimal existence provided by governmental social benefits, self-employment will have achieved a significant goal for the individual.

Ways Self-Employment Improves Quality of Life: Personal Issues

Although a primary aim of self-employment for people with disabilities is alleviating poverty for people who are unemployed and underemployed, this is not the only reason people with disabilities choose self-employment. Quality of life includes many other aspects, whether a person receives social security benefits or is financially secure. Beyond their salaries, people with disabilities desire:

- long-term employment that suits their interest and capabilities
- to learn and grow, intellectually and personally
- to have work and accomplishments that increase self-esteem
- a place in the world where their accomplishments have value
- balancing the needs created by the disabilities with productivity and independence

Beyond these goals, each individual with disabilities has personal goals that fit him or her: strengths, disabilities, family, environment, and dreams of personal achievement and self-worth.

Establishing Personal Goals for Self-Employment

To have the determination and perseverance to develop and grow a business, people need to have positive personal goals to strive for when the work gets hard, hours get long, problems occur, and success takes time or seems illusive. People with disabilities initially may have considered self-employment because they:

- have a difficult-to-impossible challenge in finding satisfying work
- see the financial potential in conventional employment as meager
- feel that they have little control over their own lives and destiny

Positive goals that are meaningful to the individual are also necessary to make self-employment a potential reality. These include goals for one's personal (and family) life as well as goals for the business. Some potential goals are included in the sections above, but there will be many others that are personal to each individual. Whatever goals are chosen, they must be meaningful, long-term goals for the person who is wanting to start the business. Goals bring focus to the business. They are the reasons for the entrepreneur to fight for success. As the business develops, meaningful goals strengthen. Additional goals also may evolve as the business takes shape.

Before starting my first business, I tried finding a job in my community that I could do, considering the limitations from my disabilities. My best prospects appeared to be part-time work, at or near minimum wage, mainly in small retail stores. I did not find the salaries enticing. Since I had ten years of business experience, I felt that office work was far more suited to my skills. I felt frustrated; my independence was lost and my self-worth greatly lowered.

I was fortunate to have a spouse who could support us financially. Prior to my illness and consequent disabilities at age thirty, I had a career and had always assumed that I could support myself independently. Now I saw no way that I could even minimally support myself, no less our two children.

Due to all of the negative factors with conventional employment, the concept of self-employment crept into my mind. But when the positive reasons appeared, the business idea started to blossom. In the beginning it was only an idea, but unemployment gives one time to work on developing the business idea and skills. It was 1984, and personal computers were new to small businesses. I found I had a skill, as well as time, to learn the business software and how it could relate to small businesses.

Few people were doing this type of work, and those who were mainly came from the computer mainframe world. Communicating with small business owners was not the strong suit for these "mainframers," but it could be mine. After some initial trial (with both success and failure), a business concept was born, with both positive personal and business goals. My personal goals included:

- staying in the business world, where I already had knowledge and value
- making people's lives better, by assisting small business owners and employees in their initial transition to computer technology. (This became a primary objective for the business, as well as a personal goal.)
- doing work that I enjoyed
- learning new skills
- experiencing personal growth

- hopefully, being a role model for my children: working hard and resolving difficult situations, despite my disabilities
- eventually, adding to the family's financial base

Each individual has his or her own dreams and goals. It is fighting for these positive goals that drives a person's energy and bolsters his or her perseverance through the challenges, uncertainty, and unforeseen difficulties of self-employment to achieve both business and personal success.

What "Entrepreneurial Risk" Means to an Individual with Disabilities

"Risk" is the word so often associated with self-employment. Chapter 1 clarified the fact that the most successful entrepreneurs take well-thought-out risks, based on extensive knowledge of their business and their market.

The degree of "financial risk" a person takes is partly based on his or her current financial situation. For many people with disabilities, financial resources are limited primarily to social security and medical insurance benefits. Keeping these benefits in place while the business is developing is essential to create financial stability for the individual. A business can take several months to a few years to consistently earn a profit. During that start-up phase, both personal and business expenses must be meet.

Understanding current guidelines and requirements of Social Security regulations is essential to avoid problems from audits, including fines, penalties, and loss of benefits. It also helps in using the programs to their fullest benefit for the person with disabilities.

A Social Security *Plan for Achieving Self Support* (PASS) and other related Social Security work incentives acknowledge the fact that for people who are classified by Social Security as blind or disabled, achieving self-support may be a gradual and ongoing process. The PASS is a part of the original supplemental security income (SSI) statute of the Social Security Act and is designed to increase a person's earning potential. A PASS allows self-employed people with disabilities to "set-aside" funds for a wide range of equipment and services related to of their business, their educational, or their personal disability-related needs.[1]

The funds set aside for PASS are excluded from SSI income and resource tests. The appropriate use of PASS plans and other Social Security work incentives can help to create a stable financial platform and greatly decrease the financial risk to people with disabilities who have limited financial resources.

Financial risks exist for all entrepreneurs when they give up or decrease salaries from conventional employment, use their savings or investments, take out business or personal loans, or bring in investors who will share in the profits. Evaluating that risk means finding the balance between the financial opportunity provided by the business and the risk involved in creating it. This evaluation should start early in the planning process, and continue through the business plan and start-up of the business.

Often a business can start in a limited and focused mode, requiring a lower initial financial investment. This method also provides time for education and experimentation through actual entrepreneurial experience. By the time the business emerges as a fully functioning enterprise, the business owners should have a much better understanding of the markets and their business. Success is more probable. Mistakes are less likely to critically damage the business. Learning the business with a limited budget forces the business owners to think more creatively, finding business methods that are effective but do not require large sums of money. This type of entrepreneurial thinking can make the difference between success and failure in the competitive world of small business ownership.

Regardless of a person's financial position, he or she must predict personal financial needs as well as the business needs for the starting months or years of the business. Personal financial forms are an essential part of the business plan. Evaluating these personal needs early can minimize painful problems in providing for living expenses while trying to get a fledgling business on its feet.

Self-Employment vs. Working Alone

Self-employment does not mean working by yourself. Chapter 1 addressed the myriad of connections that a businessperson has with other businesspeople, customers, and the general community. Even with these contacts, a person can find his or herself isolated or without adequate business or emotional support. This problem can be particularly destructive for people with disabilities, since the disabilities may create additional isolation. Working primarily in one's home also increases isolation. Isolation is usually a solvable problem when active steps are taken to provide social interaction and business support.

There are many ways to become isolated, particularly in a one-person, home business. Areas for potential isolation are many, and include:

- *Lack of contact with people who understand the same business, or related businesses.* Without this type of contact, businesspeople are less aware of changes in the industry and market. They do not have people with whom to discuss new business ideas, nor to share their business struggles and successes.
- *Lack of contact with current and potential customers* reduces the opportunity to see how well the products or services are utilized and

to find new ways to improve or expand these products or services. Isolation from customers lessens the self-satisfaction that comes from seeing your work appreciated.

- *Lack of contact with suppliers, subcontractors, and associates* can limit the potential that they can provide to a business. Some of these people function as an integral part of the business. Isolation from them limits the ability to work as a team and operate in a manner that benefits all of the parties.
- *Lack of contact with people in general* can create loneliness and depression. Some businesses can create a level of isolation where a person does not have the social contact that makes them feel a part of society, emotionally supported, and an asset to others.

Not all businesses, nor all business owners, will experience isolation. However, when continual isolation does occur, it can become a serious problem. There are many ways to alleviate isolation. The key is to work interpersonal interactions into the business operation on a regular basis. It is an important part of taking care of the business, and taking care of the business owner. One of the principal goals of self-employment for people with disabilities is integration into the community, not isolation from it.

Avoiding isolation should start with the training process. Distance learning has expanded as a teaching concept in recent years. It has the advantage of reaching people who cannot readily get to an educational institution, including many people with disabilities. It usually provides education at a reasonable price and at flexible hours, fitting people's work and personal schedules.

However, distance learning has an important downside, even when the program design is of the same caliber as a conventional college program. Distance learning lacks the face-to-face interaction that takes place in conventional college settings: in the classrooms, during student/faculty meetings, in joint student projects, and even informal student discussions.

As Wendy Grossman states in her review of distance learning in *Scientific American*, " *...most of the time learning is something that happens between people.* "[2] When dealing primarily with printed class materials, computers, and e-mail one loses the crucial learning that happens through give-and-take discussions with professors and other students. And for people with disabilities, they are starting the business planning process in isolation rather than with interaction. If distance learning is used in a business training program for people with disabilities, if should be supplemented with recurring activities. These activities must provide for discussions with persons who can

63

improve and implement the learning process and add insight into the development of the business plan.

The Role of the Person with Disabilities in the Business

All entrepreneurs need to determine what their role is in their business. Whether there is one owner, two owners, or a group of owners, each person brings his or her strengths and weaknesses into the business. If there is more than one owner, hopefully their strengths will complement each other. Regardless of the number of owners, each individual must determine what his or her role should be in the business.

It is easy to overestimate what roles an entrepreneur successfully can play in a fledgling business. It is common to underestimate the time it takes to run a business, and to underestimate the skills needed for some of the functions. For example, even simple record-keeping and bookkeeping systems need to be kept up with on a regular and accurate basis.

Without these systems, knowledge of how the business is running is muddled or lost. If government forms and taxes are not submitted on a timely basis, the business can become endangered. A person who is not comfortable with setting up these systems and maintaining them may put them on the back burner or ignore them when time and energy become an issue. Add in the time and energy absorbed by living each day with disabilities, and it is easy to see how a business can readily get out of control.

The goal for business owners is to determine where their talent and time is best spent. Then the challenge is to determine who should do the remaining work and how much money is available to pay for this work. This is not just a start-up challenge. If anything, the situation gets more complex as the company grows and the role of the owner changes with this growth.

A business can become an open pit into which unlimited amounts of time and energy are thrown. It is the job of the owner to keep this from happening. The owner must keep the focus on the essential aspects of the business. My first mentor told me that it is easy to keep busy as a business owner; the hard part is making money. Over the years I have thought about this axiom and repeated it to other businesspeople. To succeed usually requires hard work, focus, and truly understanding the business that you are in.

Prospective entrepreneurs with disabilities should use their learning time to gauge their own endurance and capabilities. If they find the needed amount of time and energy stressful, they might want to start the business on a more limited basis. Or they could see if the business can financially support more employee, vendor, or subcontractor time to supplement the entrepreneurs' capabilities. Family members might assist with the business, particularly until it becomes more profitable. The solution will fit the individual. There is no pat answer or method.

The business owner's disabilities potentially can alter his or her future role in the business. Some disabilities have the potential for gradual, intermittent, or sudden changes, reducing the business owner's ability to work. If this seems likely to occur in the future, the business plan should include procedures for keeping the business running.

These procedures may include "key" person(s), who are knowledgeable about the business, taking over some or all of the duties for the owner. (This could include, but is not limited to, business partners, employees, family members, CPA, business consultant, or a person from another company.) Without this kind of support, a business can lose the sales and income necessary to support the entrepreneur.

Able-bodied people obviously can have disabilities disrupt their businesses. In fact, a substantial percentage of business owners with disabilities started their businesses when they were non-disabled. However, for people who already have disabilities, the odds are greater that they will be affected by adverse changes in physical, psychological, or cognitive abilities. The people who work hard to build businesses want them to last into the future, regardless of changes in their bodies.

Financing the Start-Up Business

Often people with disabilities feel that they are at a disadvantage trying to get a business loan for a start-up company. Many people with disabilities have modest or very limited incomes, with social security benefits being their primary income source. They may not have personal assets that can be used as collateral for a loan. Some people with disabilities have poor credit histories due to lack of consistent employment income or heavy medical expenses. Some people with disabilities have limited work experience and no business ownership experience.

All of these factors do make it harder to get a bank loan for a start-up business. However, even the vast majority of non-disabled people who have savings, long-standing employment records, good credit, and even business experience rarely obtain start-up business loans from conventional banks. People with disabilities need to understand that they are not alone in this situation. The small percentage of start-up businesses that are able to get partial financing through bank loans usually provide substantial personal assets as collateral.

Entrepreneurs with disabilities get the financing for their businesses like most other entrepreneurs do. Money can come either from personal savings, loans from other than conventional banking sources, or from outside investment in the company. The range of options is extensive and will be discussed further in Chapter 8.

Not all options are available to a given business. Of those options that are available, the advantages must be weighed against the negative factors. Micro-loan programs often provide training and support, giving small businesses an entry to financial resources and valuable mentoring. Wise entrepreneurs will take the time to find the options that best fit their company and their personal financial situation.

Beyond loans and investments, businesses started by people with disabilities might receive funds from their department of vocational rehabilitation, especially if the money is directed toward accommodations for the disability. Departments of vocational rehabilitation also should provide assistance in finding resources for business loans. In some states, such as Wisconsin, the department of vocational rehabilitation works in conjunction with the state economic development department to combine vocational rehabilitation resources with small business loans and business training from economic development. The partnership formed by this entity became the Business Development Initiative (BDI). The BDI focuses on providing technical assistance, grants, and loans for prospective entrepreneurs with disabilities and those entrepreneurs with disabilities wishing to expand their existing businesses.[3]

Emotional Challenges of Business Ownership

In *How to Succeed on Your Own*, Karin Abarbanel describes the emotional cycle for the first eighteen months in business.[4] (The time frame may vary, depending on the amount of time spent on training, business planning, and the actual business start-up.) Although the book was written primarily for non-disabled women going from corporate positions to self-employment, it outlines a cycle of the feelings that are experienced by most people starting their own businesses.

> Stage 1: Releasing the Past
>
> Stage 2: Launching Your Venture (1 - 3 months)
> Exhilarated and Free
> Loneliness
> Image Anxiety
> Financially Fragile
>
> Stage 3: Facing Reality (4 - 6 months)
> Performance Anxiety
> Increased Tension
> Self-Doubt
> More Committed

Stage 4: Building Momentum (7 - 18 months)
　　　Stretched
　　　Financially Strained
　　　Family Tension
　　　More Knowledgeable
　　　More Focused

Being prepared for the stress and emotional changes that come with starting a business and finding strategies to deal with them means prospective entrepreneurs are more likely to succeed in their endeavors. Dealing with challenges is an ongoing process for all entrepreneurs. To begin by determining solutions for disability-related challenges is part of the learning process for reaching successful entrepreneurship.

Sources:

1. Griffin, Cary, (1999). "Rural Routes: Promising Supported Employment Practices in America's Frontier," *The Monograph of the National Supported Employment Consortium,* Richmond, VA: Virginia Commonwealth University.
2. Grossman, Wendy M., (July 1999). "Cyber View: On-Line U," *Scientific American.*
3. Verstegen, Dale and Arnold, Nancy, (1996). "The Wisconsin Business Development Program: A Partnership between the Division of Vocational Rehabilitation and the Department of Development." *Self-Employment in Vocational Rehabilitation: Building on Lessons from Rural America*, Missoula: Rural Institute/University of Montana, web site: www.ruralinstitute.umt.edu).
4. Abarbanel, Karin, (1994). *How to Succeed on Your Own*, New York: Henry Holt and Company.

- regulation classifying veteran-owned businesses as a "socially and economically disadvantaged business group," affording veteran-owned small businesses an opportunity to compete on the same level with small business concerns owned and controlled by socially and economically disadvantaged individuals.
- ability of reservist plumbers, electricians, or contractor small business owners called to active duty to access loans to keep the business afloat while the person serves the country[8]

Small Business Access and Choice for Entrepreneurs Act

Recently introduced in the US Congress, the federal Small Business Access and Choice for Entrepreneurs Act (ACE Act) could improve cost and benefits for health insurance for small businesses. The ACE Act will allow more uninsured Americans to find quality healthcare coverage by strengthening and expanding association health plans (AHP) and offering immediate 100% health insurance deductibility for the self-employed.

Currently, self-employed people can deduct only 60% of the costs of healthcare, while large businesses can deduct 100%. In 1998, Congress passed legislation to allow full deductibility in the year 2003. However, five years is a long time to self-employed people with disabilities with no healthcare coverage today.

ACE gives small businesses and self-employed individuals access to group purchasing through association health plans while giving the federal government a limited supervisory role. Costs would be managed through several key tools: strength in price negotiation, reduced administrative costs, and greater spreading of medical risk. The legislation also would strengthen the accountability of association plans and ensure better financial management and oversight of them.[9]

Assistive Technology Act

The Assistive Technology Act (ATA) goals are to:
- focus federal agencies and departments to invest in technology and technology research benefitting individuals with disabilities
- support states in sustaining and strengthening their capacity to address assistive technology needs of individuals with disabilities
- support micro-loan programs to provide assistance to individuals who desire to purchase assistive technology devices or services[10]

Although there are no specific governmental funds or loans directed to people with disabilities (with the exception of the above mentioned veterans' program), existing federal small business programs, e.g., SBA, SCORE, and Small Business Development Centers are learning more about the needs of entrepreneurs with disabilities and are functioning more pro-actively in this area.

At the state level, vocational rehabilitation (VR) is the primary agency for people with disabilities to find training and financial assistance for all types of employment, including self-employment. With the national VR system increasing its attention to small business development, more than 5,000 enterprises were helped annually by state VR departments as of 1999.[11]

Economic development programs at state, county, and local levels support new business start-ups and existing business expansion. Particularly in areas of high unemployment, business development is encouraged and supported. Government funding assists training and micro-loan programs sponsored by nonprofit organizations, usually directed at "socially and economically disadvantaged business groups.

Sources:
1. DiLeo, Dale, (1999). *Reach for the Dream,* St. Augustine, FL: Training Resource Network, Inc.
2. Reagan, Brad, (June 14, 1999). "'I Did It My Way' 101," *The Wall Street Journal.*
3. Ibid.
4. Miyares, Urban, (1996). "Actions," *Starting/Expanding a Small Business*, Bold Business Consultants web-site: www.effectivecompensation.com/bold-owners.
5. Hershey, Laura, (August 18, 1998). "Attendant Services Must Support Independence, Not Agencies," Crip Commentary, web-site: www.ourworld.compuserve.com/homepages/LauraHershey.
6. Griffin, Cary, (1999). "Rural Routes: Promising Supported Employment Practices in America's Frontier," *The Monograph of the National Supported Employment Consortium*, Richmond, VA: Virginia Commonwealth University.
7. (February 1999). "Summary of S. 33, The Work Incentives Improvement Act, Section 101(a)," *Legislative Alert: ACCSES New Legislative Action System*, American Congress of Community Support and Employment Services, web-site: accses.firminc.com.
8. Press Release, (August 6, 1999). "Important Veterans Entrepreneurship to Become Law: More than 585,000 Missouri Veterans, 24 Million Veterans Nationwide Will Benefit," House Small Business Committee: Special Projects, web-site: www.house.gov/smbiz/projects.
9. Press Release, (June 17, 1999). "Health Care Bill to Help Uninsured Passes First Hurdle to the Floor: Bill Will Help Millions of Uninsured Find Quality, Affordable Healthcare," House Small Business Committee: Special Projects, web-site: www.house.gov/smbiz/projects.
10. (May 1999). "Summary of the Assistive Technology Act, Legislative Alert: ACCSES New Legislative Action System on the American Congress of Community Support and Employment Services, web-site: accses.firminc.com.
11. Griffin, Cary, (1999). "Supporting Entrepreneurs with Disabilities" *Annual Monograph Future Designs of the Montana Consumer Controlled Careers Project*, Rural Institute/University of Montana.

> You have to have your heart in the business and the business in your heart.
>
> –THOMAS J. WATSON

Chapter 6
Owner-Oriented
Business Planning

A business plan is simply the design for starting a new business or for running an existing business. However, creating a viable business design, particularly for a new business, is neither quick nor simple. The business plan is the culmination of inspiration, evaluation, research, learning, and experimentation.

Developing the business plan for a new business typically takes several months in which ideas are examined and reworked. Finding customers and testing business options are part of the research for the business plan. When a sound business plan is designed, it becomes the blueprint for a potentially successful business.

Additionally, it serves as a baseline to measure the progress of the business. Most importantly, it is an educational tool for the entrepreneur to understand the proposed business, its market environment, and his or her role in the business. The business plan itself is not as important as what the prospective entrepreneur learns while creating the plan.

This chapter is not a "how to" manual on business plan writing. Rather, it looks at the gains in personal growth and knowledge that can be made during business planning. For those interested in knowing more about the details of business plan writing, there are references for books and web-sites on this subject in the appendix.

Individuality of the Business Plan

Each person's business plan is a unique document. The format, the organization, the length, the complexity, and the exact type of information varies from plan to plan, depending on the particular industry and the individual business.

Most plans for small business start-ups are relatively short, in the range of six to sixteen pages, including the financial statements. This is a practical length to function as a business tool. It is long enough to encompass the information needed by the business owners, but short enough to be used and reviewed readily. If more information is developed, the additional information can be kept in appendices or in separate files to support the business plan.

Professional training, consulting, and support services will be instrumental for many people developing a business plan. This does not mean that the plan is "written by outsiders for the person." The prospective entrepreneur needs to be in the center of the research and planning process, and needs to understand how the business will function. However, professional assistance can enhance the process, providing ideas, insight, and direction that the person might not be aware of on his or her own.

Ideally, the prospective entrepreneur writes the plan. If a person writes a clear and cohesive business plan, he or she probably has a sound understanding of the concepts. However, disabilities may make this difficult or impossible for some individuals. Therefore, a business consultant or counselor can do the actual writing, as long as there is direct input and understanding by the prospective business owner.

When a business plan is developed, its primary purpose should be to serve the business owners. When the plan is written primarily to obtain financial assistance or loans, the goal of guiding the owner can get lost. The business plan that truly focuses on the business and its owners is a plan that also will work well for financial goals. Although financial investment or bank financing may require an expanded business plan, this expanded plan still should use the original owner-oriented business plan as its basis.

Goals of the Owner-Oriented Business Plan

The business plan is a method for determining:
- what the prospective owner personally wants from the business
- what the goals are for the business
- what will the business accomplish
- what the owner can expect to get back from the business, and when
- what the market is for the business' service or product, and the probable sales for the business
- specifically who is, or will be, the first actual customer(s)
- if the business creates a new "niche" or uniquely satisfies an existing market need
- who the owners are, what their roles are in the business, and who will manage the business

- what operational systems should be put in place to promote the effective and consistent running of the business
- what equipment and other assets, including accommodations, will be required to effectively run the business
- what resource(s) are potentially available to finance the business
- if realistic financial projections show that the business can be run on a profitable basis over the long term
- what the goals and milestones are that can be used to measure the progress of the business

What Is Gained from the Owner-Oriented Business Plan

Creating an owner-oriented business plan teaches many lessons beyond actual business knowledge. Creating the business plan takes time and effort. It often involves discovering potential challenges, being frustrated, rethinking issues, and determining solutions. It involves finding people who can assist in developing solutions to problems.

To create the business plan, the prospective business owner must stay focused on making the business succeed. He or she must be able to keep up the enthusiasm for self-employment and for the business idea. Anyone can get off track or discouraged at some points, but the successful businessperson will be able to get back in focus and be willing to try alternative methods of developing the business.

These skills are needed throughout the life of the business. Winston Churchill's statement, *"Success is going from failure to failure without lack of enthusiasm,"* holds true for business development.

One of the goals in writing a business plan is to have the prospective businessperson decide if self-employment is the best employment alternative. However, a person who is starting a new endeavor is often vulnerable. It is easy for an advisor to dissuade a potential entrepreneur from pursuing self-employment by requiring too much in the way of business planning results, without providing that person with the proper professional business support.

Conversely, the human services worker or business consultant may be tempted to do too much of the work, allowing the entrepreneur to start the business unprepared and set up for failure. A balanced approach is needed that reflects the abilities and needs of the individual. Ideally, the same counselor or consultant should work with the person through both the business planning process and the start-up of the business.

The business planning process takes time. The tasks and time frame needed to complete the business plan should reflect the person's capabilities and disability, while keeping work on the business plan moving at a steady pace. It also should stay focused on the specific objectives for the business while making continual progress toward the completion of the plan.

Running a business takes discipline and focus, as well as time management. To have these skills, or to learn them as part of the business plan development, is an important step toward business success. The person who does not have these skills and plans to open a business needs to have a partner, key employee, or support person who can provide these abilities.

Overview of the Business Plan

Business plans have these basic elements, which are discussed in more depth below:

- Executive Summary
- Brief History of the Business Concept *and the Products and/or Services*
- Mission Statement
- Goals and Objectives
- Marketing Plan, including both market research and marketing
- Operations Plan, including accommodations for disabilities, and a human resources plan if there are employees
- Financial Plan

Business ideas come from many sources. Of course, people can create their ideas on their own. They also can have assistance from a wide range of resources:

- business consultants and advisors
- business owners in the same or related fields
- books, magazines, or Internet web-sites
- human services counselors
- friends and family members

The *Executive Summary* is a brief summary of the business plan that gives any reader a quick overview of the business.

The important point is that the business fits the prospective business owner(s). Entrepreneurs need to have a real interest in their business so that they stay enthusiastically involved through good and bad times. Additionally, each owner needs the skills to assume a definable role in the business. Although business partners, associates, employees, and vendors provide a range of skills and resources, each owner must understand his or her function and be able to perform effectively for the company.

The *Brief History of the Business Concept and the Products and/or Services* explains the business concept and how it evolved. It describes why the prospective business owner believes the business will succeed. It should reflect his or her depth of commitment to the business.

This section also tells what type of business ownership is being used and why. While many businesses start out as sole proprietorships, this is not always the best choice. It is best that this decision involves advice from a CPA for both short-term and long-term business structure and tax-related goals.

The history section also explains how the person sees him- or herself in regard to the business. It details the skills and capabilities he or she can contribute to the business, and the types of personal satisfaction and growth the person hopes to gain from the business. There should be a driving force beyond profit to start a business.

The *Mission Statement* is usually a short section that describes the owner's targeted business accomplishments. The mission statement is not only about what the owner wishes for him- or herself and the business. It includes what the owner wants for the business' customers, his or her family, specific groups of people that the business might affect, the community, or a charitable cause that the owner supports.

The *Goals and Objectives* section explains the goals of the business and the primary ways for the business to achieve these goals. Many people start out developing a business plan that encompasses numerous goals. In truth, the simpler the concept, the more likely that the business will succeed.

Businesses usually start out best with one concept, or two closely related and complementary concepts. If the research is thorough on each business concept, the entrepreneur realizes how complex and exhausting it is to go in a multitude of directions. Development of the business plan should indicate which concepts to drop, at least in the short term, and which are most likely to succeed.

As the business grows, it can take on additional concepts. But those will not necessarily be the ones that were predicted before the business opened.

The *Marketing Plan* includes researching the market and determining how to reach and sell to the market. This is often the most challenging part of a business. The businessperson must find a market that needs the proposed product or service. The owner must determine the marketing channel through which to sell the product or service, such as wholesaler, retail, catalogue, direct sales, Internet web-site, distributor, or sales representative (subcontractor.) The entrepreneur must determine competitive pricing that reflects both the cost of the product or service and the value it has to his particular market. He or she also must make reasonable assumptions regarding the geographic marketing area.

The entrepreneur must determine what makes the product or service unique or more desirable than what is already available to this market. He or she must be able to find customers who are willing to pay for the product or service. Finally, the business owner must be able to provide the product or service in a manner and at a price that entices the customers to continue the business relationship.

One of the most important lessons learned in preparing the business plan is that the customers are the central focus of the business, not the business owner. The owner is not in business until there are paying customers. The customers' needs determine additional products or services. Customers are primary "partners" in the business and must be listened to and respected. Optimally, these customers will make referrals to other potential customers or they will become positive references for the company when sales are proposed to future prospective customers.

The *Operations Plan* puts the business together physically and organizationally. It answers the questions: where will the business be located, what equipment is needed, what people will be involved, what is their place in the organization?

The Operations Plan should include accommodations for the owner's disabilities. These accommodations are not just for the physical attributes of the office, such as access, furniture, or equipment. They should take into consideration both the customers and others who will be closely associated with the business. Whether they are business partners, associates, employees, vendors, family members, or support providers, these people are an integral part of making the business work. Their role in supporting the person with a disability is integrated into their business function.

The prioritizing, timing, and costing of these operational aspects are critical to establishing the business successfully. If this planning is not done properly, the business can flounder.

Errors can occur by doing these processes too quickly or too slowly. If money is spent too quickly, for example, there may not be sufficient cash flow for day-to-day operations. If too many decisions are made before the concept of the business is clear, expensive spending errors can occur, such as signing a lease on an ineffective location or hiring employees with the wrong skills. If decisions are made too slowly, important aspects of the business may not be in place at critical times. The business owner should prioritize decisions so that there is a logical flow of information. Whenever changes are made in other parts of the business, the operational plan needs reviewing to reflect these changes.

The *Financial Plan* includes financial projections for the business for one to three years. It includes a current balance sheet if the company is already in business or has assets or debts. Assistance from a business consultant or CPA is advisable in determining financial projections.

Remember that these are "best guesses" determined from the most current information. There is no certain way of determining what the business will actually do. The financial projections provide guide posts for determining the financial success of the company, and provide warnings that changes might be needed if anticipated goals are not met.

There are a number of lessons that can be learned when developing the financial section. For instance, it becomes clear that the business must make a profit beyond the owner's salary to keep the business alive and expanding. Profit should be viewed as a major source of financing for expansion. Even if a loan is taken out for expansion, it must be paid back from profits.

Money can give the business "wiggle room" to experiment or to overcome some errors. However, money alone cannot make the business run more effectively. Starting with only a modest amount of money can make the owner think clearly about financial decisions, prioritizing, and timing expenditures. He or she might find nonfinancial or relatively economical solutions to problems, which may determine a better way to run the business in the long term.

Banks rarely make loans to start-up businesses. However, once the business is established and ready to grow, the owner wants to be able to borrow money. Since the majority of new business owners do not qualify for conventional bank loans, borrowing small amounts from micro-loan funds or other self-employment nonprofit organizations creates a track record for borrowing. When the loans are paid back in a timely manner, this early borrowing often can be expanded when future financial needs arise.

When business owners with a disability invest their own money or borrow on a repayable loan, their businesses are more likely to succeed. When people risk their own money or have a loan to repay, they work harder at achieving the goal of having a successful business. Conversely, when social services funds are available to bail business owners out of problems, the owners often do not develop the skills to run the business successfully.

Learning How to Keep from Failing

Understanding basic concepts about businesses helps companies avoid traps that can seriously harm a business venture. Learning how not to fail is as important as learning how to succeed. There are some traps that all businesses must avoid. An example from the Wharton Entrepreneurship Program illustrates this.

The Classic Start-up Pitfall

The potential entrepreneur falls in love with an idea, but does not check out whether there is a "niche."

To avoid failure:

Rule 1: Do not start working on the details of the plan before
      determining who is going to buy the product or service.

Rule 2: Focus your efforts on what can succeed.[1]

87

Each industry has its own rules and requirements for making a profit and becoming successful. Each individual business must determine its own strategies for success. These lessons usually take time, research, and experience. Businesses that take the time to learn and to grow gradually have a far greater chance of reducing errors and recovering from misjudgments or risks than companies that try to start out at full speed. To shortcut this kind of learning and experience can be devastating to a start-up or growing small business.

Avoiding pitfalls will not guarantee any specific level of success. However, knowledge of potential pitfalls, combined with careful monitoring of the business and the business plan, will keep most businesses from failing.

Source:
1. *Small Businesses Series* (October 1996), CNBC.

CASE STUDY III
Halsey Store Maintenance:
Business Plan Summary

Halsey Store Maintenance is a sole proprietorship located in Libby, Montana. It will provide local merchants the service of having professional care of the sidewalks in front of their businesses. Sweeping, washing, and snow removal is offered under contracted services. Each merchant will have a choice of day and time their walks will be serviced. The goals of this business are:
1. quality, friendly, and satisfying care of sidewalks
2. enhancing the overall appearance of Libby, therefore enhancing the tourist trade
3. enabling me, as the owner, to realize my dream of being self-supporting

The business initially will consist of contracting with ten downtown merchants to maintain the sidewalks in front of their stores. I will grow my business at a steady rate, careful not to take on more work than I can handle. My goal is to have thirty businesses under contract at the end of a three-year period.

Considering my strong work ethic and my involvement with community organizations, I feel confident that Halsey Store Maintenance will prosper. This business will grow and weave into the fabric of the rural community of Libby, Montana, and will succeed because of my true affection for it.

Background

Halsey Store Maintenance will be successful partly due to the lack of services offered in this area. Acting on a suggestion of the superintendent of service for the City of Libby, Montana, I have surveyed the businesses on the main street and found many of them are in need of someone to sweep and wash their sidewalks in the spring, summer, and fall and to remove snow in the winter. Since I am well-known in our small community, the merchants know and trust me to do a good job and be dependable.

The Libby county unemployment rate is 8.8%, and is third highest in Montana. Jobs are very hard to come by. The jobs I have had, dishwasher and janitor, do not offer the financial stability I need for my future. My dream is to be able to afford a family and a home one day. I cannot achieve my dream on a minimum wage job that offers ten to fifteen hours per week.

I have worked at some type of job since I was five years old. Hard work is not new to me. Over the past years I have searched for a living-wage job. There are none available to me. If I am to remain in my home town and enjoy the support system of family and friends, being self-employed is my best option in attaining my dream. Owning my own business would allow me to benefit from my strong work ethic plus the advantage of flexibility and independence. My self-esteem is growing as I prepare for my business.

Mission and Goals

My mission is to earn a living-wage job in order to achieve my dream of owning a home and having a family. The second part of my mission is to help Libby's economy. Keeping the sidewalks clean and free of snow helps create pride. It makes Libby more inviting to people passing through. We have festivals and events that bring people to town, and if we improve the appearance of our town, people will stay longer and spend more money.

My personal objective is to become profitable quickly through the conservative, planned, and steady development of Halsey Store Maintenance operating successfully in all four seasons in Libby, while contributing to the beautification and maintenance of my community. I will begin with ten businesses. I will set aside 35% of my income for income taxes. At the end of the first year, I will hire an accountant to prepare my taxes.

My long-term plans are to take Halsey Store Maintenance from a small operation servicing ten businesses to a living-wage job of servicing thirty businesses per week which equals $150.00 weekly, or $600.00 monthly. If I can retain all thirty businesses throughout the winter for snow removal, my income will double during December, January, and February due to higher wages for snow removal. The second $600.00 per month (the cost of leasing my snow blower) will be to pay maintenance and operation of snow equipment and replacement as equipment wears out. My projection for thirty customers under contract is three years.

If the economy of Libby improves and more merchants can afford my services, I would like to hire my friend, also an individual with disabilities, to work for me. The service I offer not only gives me a job that I really like doing and am very good at, it also makes my community more favorable to the tourist trade and instills pride in the appearance of Libby. Libby is in the most beautiful setting in Montana. I want the town to be as attractive as the area that surrounds it.

Services

Services offered through my business will be sweeping and washing sidewalks in the spring, summer, and fall. During the winter I will remove snow from the sidewalks. I offered merchants the service of removing weeds and alley cleanup during the summer months when the city was enforcing the ordinance of overgrown vegetation. Some of the merchants hired me, others did the work themselves. In both cases it was a benefit to our city. I will continue to offer that service when time allows.

I anticipate two slow business times, early spring and late fall. During those times I will do occasional jobs for merchants that use my services on a regular basis. Because of the relationships formed with them maintaining the sidewalks, I think they will be willing to hire me for occasional jobs.

Halsey Store Maintenance Balance Sheet

ASSETS

CURRENT ASSETS:

Cash	52.00
Accounts Receivable	-0-
Total Current Assets	52.00

FIXED ASSETS:

Equipment	804.49
Less Accumulated Depreciation	(402.25)
Total Fixed Assets	402.24
TOTAL ASSETS	**454.24**

LIABILITIES & EQUITY

CURRENT LIABILITIES:

Accounts Payable	-0-
Total Current Liabilities	-0-

LONG TERM LIABILITIES:

Long Term Debt	-0-
Total Long Term Liabilities	-0-

EQUITY:

Owner's Equity	52.00
Retained Earnings	402.24
Total Owner's Equity	**454.24**
TOTAL LIABILITIES & EQUITY	**454.24**

FINANCIAL NOTE: The cost of running Halsey Store Maintenance is modest, with the main expenses being: inexpensive supplies; repairs, maintenance, and replacement of equipment; and limited advertising. The out-of-pocket expenses (excluding taxes) are usually between $100 to $200 per month.

Personnel

Halsey Store Maintenance will be run by me. In the future I will hire an accountant-secretary and possibly another employee. Our college offers adult basic education with one-on-one instruction. I can learn a simple bookkeeping system that will satisfy the needs of my business for now. I plan to draw on my support system for assistance. My friends, family, and job coach will continue to support my efforts in self-employment.

Marketing

Word of mouth will be a large part of marketing my business. I plan to circulate flyers by hand, list my business in the yellow pages of the phone book, run ads occasionally in the local paper, and take advantage of a very affordable radio program. I will offer discount incentives to my customers and occasionally a drawing for a "free one-time" service. I will publish my customers' names in a newsletter put out by Achievements, Inc. (Achievements, Inc., is a training facility for adults with developmental disabilities) and ask that readers patronize the businesses listed. I will show my customers the newsletter. The Chamber of Commerce is including information about my business in their newsletter, which goes out to three hundred businesspeople.

Competition

At this time there is no competition in the business area where I plan to concentrate my efforts. In a small town where unemployment is high, others might imitate my efforts when they see me succeeding. I plan to endear myself to my customers with excellent customer service and reasonable prices. I plan to be well-established before the competition has a chance to form a similar business.

Having researched what the merchants are willing to pay compared to the length of required work time, I have calculated a fair and reasonable price. I am a fast worker and can average $10.00 per hour of actual work time. That does not include the time it takes to move from one location to another. (I am trying to line up customers as close to each other as possible, and ideally an entire block will use my service.) When I am using a snow blower, I will double my price. My pricing structure takes into account the expenses that make up my overhead, including upkeep on equipment and depreciation at a rate that allows for replacement of tools and equipment as needed.

Personal Reflections from Keven Halsey

I think it takes the following to make a business successful:
- I believe that hard work is necessary for small business success. I like to work hard, and have worked hard since I was a child.
- I feel that doing a good job for customers is also necessary for success. In order to do the quality of work that I feel my customers deserve, I often get up at 5 am so that I have enough time to clear and clean the walks in front of my customers' stores before their businesses open. I make sure that I am on time and that my customers know they can depend on me.

I get other things from my business besides money:
- The business allows me to get out into the community, where I am able to be with other businesspeople.
- My customers are happy with my work and with me personally. Their respect and friendship make me feel good about myself and give me confidence and self-assurance.
- Although the business as yet does not provide my full income, I am happy that I made the decision to start my own business.

How to keep the business running during slow periods:
* [Like many beginning entrepreneurs, Keven has a conventional job while working to establish his business.] I have a part-time job with Achievements, Inc., that provides me with income in addition to my business income. Because I am willing to work hard, I do not have a problem working at both the job at Achievements, Inc., and running my own business.

In writing his business plan, Halsey had assistance from Dave Hammis from the Rural Institute-University of Montana and a job coach from a human services agency that works with people with developmental disabilities, Achievements, Inc. Another job coach from Achievements, Inc., provides ongoing assistance with his business.

Material for this case study has been taken from the Halsey Store Maintenance business plan and an interview with Keven Halsey. The business plan material has been edited to fit the format of this book; consequently, it does not contain all of the information in the original business plan. Most notably, financial planning and projects are not included here.

Chapter 7
Debunking Business Planning Misconceptions

This chapter addresses several of the misconceptions and myths that can arise regarding the planning and creation of businesses owned by people with disabilities. When these misconceptions persist and affect the business planning process, they place substantial hurdles in the paths of entrepreneurs with disabilities who seek success and self-reliance. There always will be people who believe these misconceptions. It is important that businesspeople with disabilities and the people who are supporting them in their entrepreneurial endeavors know the facts.

Company Sizes

Misconception: People with disabilities can only handle one- or two-person businesses.

Fact: Although the majority of businesses owned by people with disabilities have few employees, some entrepreneurs with disabilities own larger businesses, employing a substantial number of workers.

A striking example of this situation comes from the *1996 Directory of Business Owners with Disabilities: Resource Guide,* published by the Disability Community Small Business Development Center in Ann Arbor, Michigan.[1] 158 businesses listed their number of employees in the directory. Twenty-nine percent have three to ten employees and 10% have eleven employees or more.

The following table compares all of the companies listed in the Michigan Directory with US Census statistics for companies with fifty or less employees, taken from the 1992 Economic Census.[2]

Table 1
Michigan Directory: 1992 Economic Census
Size of Business

Company Size	Owners with Disabilities	All Small Businesses
1 to 4 employees	75 %	58 %
5 to 9 employees	12 %	22 %
10 to 19 employees	10 %	12 %
20 to 50 employees	3 %	8 %

Although the companies from the *Michigan Directory* were smaller than those measured in the economy at large, the business sizes followed a pattern similar to the general population. Since the Disability Community Small Business Development Center in Ann Arbor had only supported business development for people with disabilities for a few years, as a group these were "younger" businesses than those reported by the census. It is probable that the size profiles would be more alike if the ages of the businesses could be accounted for.

Types of Businesses

Misconception: People with disabilities can handle only simple, home-based businesses, comparable to low-level jobs that they are often offered in conventional employment.

Fact: The types of businesses that people with disabilities own is expansive. The following table shows the categories of businesses listed in the Michigan Directory. The range and scope of these businesses truly demonstrate that creativity and diversity of ideas thrives with entrepreneurs with disabilities. (See Table 2.)

The *Montana/Wyoming Careers Through Partnerships Project*[3] also illustrates the diversity of types of businesses started by people with disabilities. This a US Department of Labor initiative to help people with disabilities reenter the workforce. The Rural Institute Training Department at the University of Montana worked collaboratively with the Montana Job Training Partnership on this project. The objective was to provide the participants with "choice" in regard to their employment goals and "flexibility" of methods for reaching those goals. Half of the participants elected self-employment. As Table 3 on page 98 shows, a wide range of businesses were developed by this group of entrepreneurs with disabilities.

Costs for Self-Employment/Business Start-Ups

Misconception: It is more costly for a person with disabilities to start a business than to be trained to enter or reenter the work force through conventional employment.

Table 2
Michigan Directory: 1992 Economic Census
Types of Business

- Advertising
- Appliance/Electronic Sales and Service
- Automotive Sales and Service
- Business Brokerage/Real Estate
- Business Services
- Clerical Services
- Clothing & Crafts
- Computer Sales/Service/Training
- Consulting Services for People with Disabilities
- Contractors/Builders/Excavators
- Creative Services
- Desktop Publishing/Printing
- Engravings/Awards
- Entertainment & Recreation
- Environmental Services
- Food/Eating Establishments
- Janitorial/Cleaning Supplies
- Landscaping/Snow Removal/Lawn Care
- Manufacturing
- Medical Supplies/Services
- Products/Services for People with Disabilities
- Professional Services/Accounting
- Temp Employment Services/Light Assembly
- Travel/Transportation
- Woodworking

Fact: The Montana/Wyoming Careers through Partnerships Project provides quantitative evidence to debunk this misconception. Table 3 clearly shows that most of the start-up companies were developed at a relatively reasonable cost of between $3,500 to $6,000. In fact, the average cost to start a business in the Montana/Wyoming Project was $4,112, slightly less than the $4,281 cost for project participants choosing conventional employment.

The self-employment funding and services came from a number of resources. Therefore costs were spread over a number of government and non-profit resources:

1. Job Training Partnership Act (JTPA)
2. Vocational Rehabilitation
3. Social Security Work Incentives (PASS)
4. Micro-Loans for Business
5. Small Business Administration
6. Lump Sum Payment of Unemployment Benefits

Although the participants and their families were not able to contribute money to the business start-ups, many participants had family members who became an integral part of the business. The family members provided

Table 3

Business Starts Montana Careers Through Partnership Project : 1998-99

Employment Goal	Assets Purchased	Supports Purchased	Total $
1. Desktop Publishing	Computer, Software, Scanner, Fax	Job Coach	$ 5,576
2. Glass Installation	Tools, Computer, Advertising, Rentals	Job Coach	$10,352
3. Wood Carving	Woodworking Tools	Job Coach/VR Customer	$ 3,818
4. Lawn Care, Snow Removal	Equipment, Clothing, Advertising	Job Coach/VR Customer	$ 1,712
5. Internet Research Service	Clothing, Advertising, Printer, Internet Service, Car Repair	Job Coach/VR Customer	$ 4,882
6. Medical Billing Service	Software, Liability, Fax, Computer, Advertising	Job Coach	$ 6,017
7. Medical Billing Service	Computer, Auto Repair	Job Coach	$ 3,703
8. Computer Repair	Computer, Printer	Job Coach	$ 2,119
9. Custom Embroidery	Software	Job Coach/VR Customer	$ 1,402
10. Lawn Care Snow Removal	Tolls, Equipment, Advertising		$ 3,615
11. Wood Working	Tools, Advertisement	Job Coach/VR Customer	$ 3,717
12. Online Marketing	Computer, Scanner, Camera, Printer, Software	Entrepreneurial Skills Occupational Skills	$ 7,377
13. Wood Working	Tools	Job Coach	$ 4,756
14. Dog Biscuit Manufacture	Equipment, Supplies, Advertising	Job Coach	$ 5,780
15. Computer Service	Equipment, Supplies, Advertising	Job Coach	$ 5,633
16. Rocky Mountain Guitars	Tools, Equipment	Job Coach	$ 4,581
17. House Cleaning Business	Occupational Skills	Entrepreneurial Skills Job Coach/VR Customer	$ 4,376
18. Web/Desktop Publishing	Computer, Software	Occupational Skills	$ 5,370
19. Home Inspection Service	Tools, Equipment	Occupational Skills Entrepreneurial Skills Job Coach	$ 5,512
20. Therapeutic Touch		Entrepreneurial Skills Occupational Skills Job Coach	$ 5,500
21. Secretarial	Computer, Scanner, Printer, Fax	Entrepreneurial Skills Occupational Skills Job Coach/VR Customer	$ 5,000
22. Used Clothing Store	Housing, Phone	Entrepreneurial Skills Occupational Skills Job Coach	$ 5,500
23. Sign & Graphic	Computer, Software, Plotter	Entrepreneurial Skills Job Coach	$ 3,850
24. Lawn Maintenance Service	Tools, Equipment	Entrepreneurial Skills Job Coach	$ 3,850
25. Tavern	Pending	Entrepreneurial Skills Job Coach	$ 1,800
26. Office Aquatics	Tools, Equipment, Advertising	Assessments Entrepreneurial Skills Job Coach/VR Customer	$ 6,600
27. Food Service	Transportation, Uniform, Insurance	Job Coach/VR Customer	$ 1,017
28. Food Service	Transportation, Uniform, Insurance	Job Coach/VR Customer	$ 1,017
29. Food Service	Transportation, Uniform, Insurance	Job Coach/VR Customer	$ 1,017
30. Food Service	Transportation, Uniform, Insurance	Job Coach/VR Customer	$ 1,017
31. Food Service	Transportation, Uniform, Insurance	Job Coach/VR Customer	$ 1,017

more than their labor and their professional skills. They were partners to the entrepreneurs with disabilities, often with complementary capabilities and approaches to the business. As both family members and partners, they offered strong emotional support and commitment to the ongoing success of the business.[4] Even family members who are only peripherally associated with the business can give the emotional support that is so essential when a person with disabilities is starting a new venture.

Self-Employed Subcontractor vs. Conventional Employee
Misconceptions:
1. An employer can readily hire "subcontractors" instead of employees in order to avoid paying payroll taxes.
2. An individual can find work more easily if he or she works as a subcontractor rather than an employee.

Fact: Under both federal and state regulations, there are many limitations regarding who is considered a subcontractor.

Even experienced businesspeople are not always clear on the difference between self-employed persons working as subcontractors and those considered employees. This is because the federal government does not define subcontractor specifically, so it is open to variable interpretation. At the time this book is written, the US Department of Labor has over twenty "tests" for a person to qualify as a subcontractor. Additionally, each state can make its own determination of what constitutes an employee.

It is often tempting either to start a small business functioning as a subcontractor to a larger business, or to start hiring workers as subcontractors. Although these can be good business strategies, diligence is required in order to stay within the government guidelines. Not following these guidelines can cost a business substantial amounts of money, sometimes closing down the business. If the government determines an employee-employer relationship exists, it will want to recoup the appropriate payroll taxes, plus interest, plus penalties. Neither the primary business nor the subcontractor is immune from this action, and the government is not likely to forgive the infraction and give the business a second chance.

To be safe, start with the assumption that the federal and state governments want workers to be employees whenever possible. Also assume that the government thinks that if the worker looks like an employee and acts like an employee, he or she is an employee.

Briefly, if the person works for only one company, he or she is functioning as an employee. Even if the person works for more than one company, but a specific company controls the worker's hours or how the worker does the work, that person is acting as an employee of that company. It does not matter if the person works at home, or another location outside of the business. The government can still consider the person an employee.

99

There are many other constraints, depending on the type of business and the particular job. If there is any concern whether a person is an employee or a subcontractor, consult with a CPA or a legal advisor knowledgeable about small businesses. The federal and state governments provide information on this subject, but it is not always understandable without professional assistance.

There are often overlooked but important factors that the person with disabilities needs to know before hiring a subcontractor or becoming a subcontractor. The following are two key considerations that could have extremely detrimental consequences if they are not properly understood:

1. If the person with disabilities is the business owner hiring subcontractors, he or she must report the money paid to each subcontractors on a 1099 form. There also may be payments and reporting for workers' compensation insurance. It is advisable to have professional accounting assistance the first time that subcontractors are hired and when their income is reported.

2. If the person with disabilities is the subcontractor, he or she needs to understand that the company using his or her services will not be withholding income tax and will not be making deposits for FICA or Medicare. As the subcontractor, the person with disabilities is responsible for paying his or her income tax, including quarterly tax deposits, and paying both the employer and employee portions for FICA and Medicare. Professional accounting assistance is highly recommended to understand the financial obligation, the timing for payments, and the potential fines and penalties when payments are not made at the proper time and for the correct amount.

Business Structures and Ownership

The terms "self-employment," "business structures," and "ownership" are often misunderstood and misused in ways that can be harmful to the business and its owners. This section explains some of the facts concern self-employment, business structures, and ownership, with the goal of helping to make these complex concepts more understandable and usable for entrepreneurs with disabilities. The primary considerations for choosing a business structure are its effects on the:

- taxation of the business and its owners
- ability to obtain financing for the business
- SSI and/or SSDI payments to the business owners
- liability of the business and its owners

Liability can be limited, but it cannot be eliminated in cases such as personal bad acts or criminal actions; personal guarantees on business loans; professional actions by lawyers, doctors, or accountants; and specific state laws requiring personal liability for corporate shareholders, officers, or board members.

Since there can be additional considerations, each business owner must look at his or her individual situation and needs before deciding what is the best choice for the business. With so many complex issues involved, it is highly recommended to use a CPA who is knowledgeable in small business matters for information, guidance, and recommendations. If SSI or SSDI payments or PASS plans are involved, expertise in these areas also is recommended. In certain situations, legal counsel also may be advisable.

Types of Business Structures

Sole Proprietorships

This is the quickest and easiest business structure to adopt. If the owner doesn't incorporate and doesn't have a partner, he or she is automatically a sole proprietor. Legally, the owner and the business are the same. For a sole proprietor, the net profit is taxed at personal income tax rates and the owner is personally liable for any debts or losses that incur.

Misconception: In human services settings, a sole proprietorship often is seen as a one-person, home business. The owner is often thought of in terms of working alone, doing everything for the business.

Fact #1: Although this is conceptually possible, an isolated business owner is pragmatically a likely candidate for failure. Additionally, being isolated is emotionally very stressful over an extended period of time, which in itself can cause failure. Having disabilities often creates a level of isolation that is difficult to tolerate, without increasing this isolation by working alone at home with limited contacts.

Fact #2: A sole proprietor is a single owner of a business. It is the only type of business ownership that allows a single owner. This does not limit the number of employees or the location of the business.

Additionally, the owner can and should have outside resources that are related to and support the business, such as suppliers, a CPA, referral or marketing resources, a network of people with similar interests, and customers, to name a few. The principle business location, or a secondary office, can be in the home. However, to run the business, serve customers, keep up with the industry, and make sales, there must be outside contact. The individual business owner rarely does all of the functions. Employees and outside resources handle any number of these functions. The owner needs to keep in contact with those resources in order to manage the business successfully.

Misconception: All small businesses should start as sole proprietorships.

Fact: A sole proprietorship scenario is usually the best choice for the start-up business if it:
- does not need a large capital investment
- does not have significant liabilities
- has limited profits (or losses) in the initial stage of development

If that is the case, there may not be a need to bother with the expense and time of creating a corporation or partnership. However, if a sole proprietorship does not meet all three of these conditions, another business structure might fit the company better. Additionally, all businesses have different attributes that may move the company toward a different business structure even when it meets the above conditions.

Partnerships

A partnership often is used to create a company in which the owners have complementary and necessary skills for making the business a success. It can also serve as a means for bringing needed financial capital into the business.

Partnerships can be formal, with each party having a share of the ownership in the business. These formal arrangements can have a variety of business structures, including corporate structures. There are also less formal partnerships, where individuals outside of the business or from other companies work together when it is beneficial for all of the parties involved. Such informal agreements can be short-term, possibly relating to a single business opportunity.

Informal partnerships also can serve long-term business goals. A group of companies with complementary products or services can combine to increase their ability to provide a wider range of products or services. Each business stays focused on what they do best, but the consortium enables each business to satisfy its customer's broader needs. Additionally, the company benefits by expanding its own market base.

Key employees often take on a partnership role in running a business, regardless of whether they have an actual ownership interest in the company. Providing them with ownership is an incentive for them to stay with the company. For example, it is often advantageous for an entrepreneur with disabilities to have a non-disabled business partner who can provide complementary and supportive physical, or cognitive, or emotional skills.

In a general partnership, owners share the business burden. It usually costs less and is easier to form than a corporation. Requirements vary between and within states. County clerk's offices will have the specific requirements. Annual partnership returns tell the IRS and the state how much the partnership earned or lost, and how the gains and losses are divided among the partners.

The downside of partnerships is that each owner is personally responsible for the other partner's liabilities related to the business. One partner can take actions - such as signing a contract - that legally bind the partnership entity, even if all the partners were not consulted. Each partner also is liable personally for injuries caused by one partner on company business. A partnership can protect itself against such risks by carrying the proper insurance. Creating a written general partnership agreement that protects all parties is highly recommended. Without a formal agreement there is little flexibility or protection. Benefits: Provides a way to share the business burden; has simpler paperwork and less cost than incorporation.

Misconception: Partnerships always are made up by an active business relationship between two people who know each other very well.

*Fact: Th*is perception of partnership often comes from an individual's limited personal experience in this area, or from exposure to TV or motion pictures. There are many types of partnerships, each providing attributes that can be beneficial or detrimental to a specific business or individual. Partners can be active or passive, and be fully open to liability or be limited, just to name a few variations. Each type of partnership has advantages and disadvantages, depending on the taxation, liability, or capitalization needs of the business and the partners. Additionally, partnership can range in size from two owners in one location to numerous owners in multiple locations.

For instance, one can also form a special kind of partnership called a limited partnership. These typically are used in situations where a business wants to finance expansion. A limited partnership must have one or more general partners who have the same responsibilities and liability restrictions as they would in a general partnership. But in addition, there are one or more "limited" partners, typically investors not involved in the day-to-day activities of the company. These limited partners are not liable personally for debts of the partnership, and they get the same tax advantages as a general partner. However, they do have significant restrictions. They cannot be involved in the management of the company (with few exceptions). If they are, they may become personally liable for the partnership's debts.

Creating a limited partnership can be as complex and costly as forming a corporation. An attorney should assist in conforming to various filing requirements for the state.

Corporations
S Corporation

S Corporation status provides the liability protection of a corporation, and taxation on the same basis as a partnership. However, some states tax an S corporation in the same manner as a C corporation, so one must be knowledgeable of the state regulations. Many tax experts recommend S corporation status for smaller entities and start-ups. If a business experiences a loss in its first years, the losses generally pass through to the owner's personal income tax return. The disadvantages to a start-up business can be additional paperwork and expenses as compared to a sole-proprietorship. There are no benefit deductions for employee-owners with 2% or more of corporate stock.

C Corporation

C corporations are considered separate entities from their shareholders, and must pay taxes on income left over after business expenses. Owners of a C corporation run the risk of being taxed twice on the profits - once as a corporation, and a second time as an individual if profits are dispensed as dividends or the corporation is liquidated. However, many tax and financial experts can come up with ways to plan for profits to avoid or limit this type of double taxation. There are a number of instances where it is beneficial to become a C corporation. If the business plans to keep profits and other sizable amounts of cash to finance growth, repay debt, or make other capital expenditures, C corporation status makes sense because C corporations can take advantage of the lower initial corporate income tax rates. For profitable companies, C corporation status can provide greater flexibility in terms of planning and controlling federal income taxes. C corporations also can deduct the full cost of certain fringe benefit packages, although deductions of premiums paid for health insurance are increasing for sole proprietors, partnership, and S Corporations:

Calendar Year	Deduction
1999 through 2001	60%
2002	70%
2003 and thereafter	100%

Misconception: Corporate structures are best only for larger businesses.

Fact: A corporation needs only two persons, who are both corporate officers and board members. These people can be family members. Only one of these people needs to be an active employee of the business. The second person can do the limited work of officer and board member for a few hours per year. There are numerous variations in corporate stock programs that can provide benefits for a business and its owners.

Another approach is the Limited Liability Company (LLC). The LLC is a hybrid of the corporation and the partnership. While the liability safeguards are similar to those of a corporate shareholder, the owners pay taxes like a partnership on their personal tax returns. The LLC has more flexibility than an S corporation or a limited partnership. Although most states allow limited liability companies, restrictions can vary. Check with the state department of taxation to find out the applicable state laws. Filing to form an LLC can be extremely complicated; using an attorney is advised.

There are other business structures that suit specific needs, such as professional corporations or nonprofit corporations. For information on these structures, and additional information on business structures in general, visit the American Express web-site at www.americanexpress.com/homepage/smallbusiness.shtml and click on "Creating an Effective Business Plan."

Changing Business Structures

Misconception: Once a business structure is chosen, a company does not need to concern itself with this matter again.

Fact: The business structure a company chooses at the start does not need to be a permanent selection.

For example, businesses that begin by testing the waters on a very limited scale often find the sole proprietorship to be an appropriate business structure. That way one can start using the simplest business structure and see what direction the business takes. Later the owner may find it advantageous to change to a type of partnership or corporation. Factors that encourage a change in business structure include, but are not limited to: company profit increases affecting taxes, increases in financial liability, the need for business loans, and the need for additional capital investments. (See the box "Business Structures" on page 18 for examples.)

Tax Example

A sole proprietorship is successful and has a $35,000 profit at the end of the year. This amount goes directly into the individual's personal tax return, where he or she must pay self-employment tax of 15.3% (current rate in the year 2000) or $5,355. Additionally, the $35,000 becomes part of the individual's income subject to federal and state income taxes. Changing to a different business structure can help to mitigate this tax burden.

Business Loan Example

Banks generally are less willing to loan money to sole proprietorships than to S corporations, even when their financial situations are identical. Banks will require the owners of both sole proprietorships and S corporations to provide personal guarantees for business loans, so there is no difference in the risk for the bank. However, banks generally have experienced higher default rates from sole proprietorships. Therefore, banks are more reluctant to loan money to them.

S corporations are more acceptable loan risks because owners of S corporations are required by law to keep more detailed and consistent financial records. Consequently, S corporations are more aware of and more responsive to the financial situation of the business. They are less likely to have financial problems that will cause them to default on their loans.[5]

Finding Partners and Corporate Owners

Misconception: If I get along with a individual on a personal basis, and we both have interests and abilities to bring to the business, we will have a solid business partnership.

Fact #1: Bringing together partners or corporate owners always has risks at the level of personal interaction.

Business partners need to each have an appropriate role in the company that is understood by all concerned. This role may be as a passive investor or an active participant in the day-to-day working of the business. The specific duties for each partner should suit the needs of the business and be complementary to the skills provided by the other partners. The goal is to be supportive and synergistic, and to avoid creating power struggles and control battles.

Fact #2: Partners need to be able to work together on an extended basis and under stressful conditions.

Additionally, partners need to agree on how to divide company revenues, work load, and expenses. This is a far different relationship than one normally has with a family member, life partner, friend, or business associate. It is important to find ways to work comfortably with business partners, particularly if your partner is also a person with whom you live.

Having physically separated workspace can help significantly. In my work situation, my husband (and partner) works at our business office, while I work out of my home office. I am connected directly to the company computer network, and communicate through e-mail, fax, and telephone. My husband "couriers" mail and other materials between the main office and my home office. It is a work relationship that permits us to be business partners, but have personal space and autonomy.

It is important to take time to assess if a suitable relationship is possible prior to creating a formal partner agreement or a corporation. Breaking these agreements can be both financially and emotionally painful.

Tax Issues

Misconceptions: Taxes for sole proprietorships are straightforward. The business owner or a "friend" can do the taxes. You just take the business invoices and receipts to the tax preparer at the end of the year.

Fact #1: Tax issues for businesses and business owners can be complex. To avoid problems and utilize tax benefits, CPAs should provide advice:
- before major business and financial decisions are made
- for both business and personal tax planning
- for business and personal tax preparation
- on any question regarding finances, taxes, regulator agencies, or any situation where there might be confusion or uncertainty regarding a financial issue

Fact #2: Taking the business invoices and receipts to the tax preparer to sort out at the end of the year is an expensive way to do bookkeeping.

Also, information that is not recorded and filed on a regular basis can get lost or mis-categorized. Most importantly, the business' financial activity is not examined closely until the end of the year. By that time, the business owner may have made costly mistakes that could have been prevented if he or she had received timely financial reports.

Rural Business Myths

In 1994 researchers from twelve universities conducted a survey[6] that included rural retailers from Iowa, Illinois, Indiana, Kansas, Louisiana, Michigan, Nebraska, North Dakota, Ohio, Oklahoma, Wisconsin, and Wyoming. The study was developed to identify successful small rural retailers and characteristics that they had in common. The goal was to debunk negative myths concerning the prospects for rural retail businesses. Some of the findings are summarized on the next page.

Myth #1: Rural retailers are not profitable.
Fact: High-profit retailers in the study reported profits of 17% or more. This is higher than high-profit retailers reported in Dun and Bradstreet.

Myth #2: Big is better – or, at least, more profitable.
Fact: High-profit retailers had the lowest sales volume of the three groups. Small businesses are more flexible and are able to react quickly to changes in the competitive environment.

Myth #3: It pays to advertise.
Fact: Advertising is beneficial, but it should not be excessive. All categories of retailers paid a very small percentage of sales for advertising.

Myth #4: High inventory turnovers lead to profitability.
Fact: The most profitable retailers did not have a higher inventory turnover than the least profitable retailers. The turnovers for rural retailers were lower than those for any categories of retailers presented in Dun and Bradstreet.

Myth #5: Profitable firms use other people's money.
Fact: Two ratios, current liabilities to net worth and total liabilities to net worth, show that high-profit firms are not "borrowed up" – they have the lowest figures for these ratios.

Myth #6: Location, location, location.
Fact: Although location always can impact a business, high-density, urban locations are not necessary to turn a profit. Rural retailers paid less than one-fourth the rent of urban retailers, helping to balance the lower traffic levels with significantly lower cost for space.

Myth #7: All small businesses are cash-poor.
Fact: Successful rural retailers are not cash-poor. Even when inventory is removed from the equation (quick ratio), the high-profit firms remained at the one-to-one ratio, indicating adequate ability to meet financial obligations.

Myth #8: It is more expensive to run a small business than a big business.
Fact: The rural retailers in all three of the categories had lower total expenses (high-profit = 23%; medium-profit = 29%; low-profit =33%) than did the urban retailers (41%).

Myth #9: You have to discount to be profitable.
Fact: High-profit retailers had a gross margin of 44%. The least profitable firms in the study had the lowest markup (3%). Small businesses cannot compete on price. Instead, the small business' edge is a combination of flexibility, unique merchandise, and superb customer service.

The Business World Is Full of Myths and Misconceptions

In planning and creating a successful business, it is important to separate the truth from the myths and so-called conventional wisdom. Each type of enterprise, each location, and each business owner brings unique situations, challenges, and capabilities to the a prospective business. Planning and creating a successful business is a challenge to any businessperson. When an entrepreneur with disabilities takes on this difficult task, his or her prospective business should be assessed as a unique endeavor. Prejudice or ignorance have no place in this process.

Sources:
1. *1996 Directory of Business Owners with Disabilities: Resource Guide*, Disability Community Small Business Development Center, 2568 Packard Rd., Ann Arbor, MI 48104, 303-971-0277.
2. 1992 Economic Census: Enterprise Statistics, web-site: Statistics about Small Business and Large Business from the Census Bureau, www.census.gov/epcd/www/smallbus.html.
3. Shelley, Roger, Hayes, Tom, Newman, Lisa, and Griffin, Cary, (1999). "A New Formula for Success in Montana: Choice + Flexibility," Bringing *Home the Bacon, Inventive Self-Employment & Supported Employment in Rural America*. Missoula: Rural Institute/University of Montana.
4. Personal communication with Roger Shelly of the Rural Institute/University of Montana (1999).
5. Personal communication with Robert Arnold, CPA, with Roger Nittler and Co., Inc., Denver, Colorado (1999).
6. *Rural Myths: MSU Extension Small Business Bulletin - NCR5550111.*

> There are no secrets to success. It is the result of preparation, hard work, learning form failure.
>
> – COLIN POWELL

Chapter 8
Business Planning: Addressing Business Challenges

Planning and developing a new business venture is far more than a "paper-and-pencil" task. There is an incredible amount of hands-on learning in creating a small business. Creating a sound business plan may require the entrepreneur's interactions with customers, vendors, associates in related businesses, accountants, lawyers, bankers, government agencies, competitors, and employees. Entrepreneurs with disabilities need to get in contact with these resources in order to obtain knowledge and insight for the development of their business.

Running a successful business is a dynamic and continually changing process. The actual start-up of the business is just one of many milestones in developing, managing, and growing a business. Effective business planning does not just focus on the "start-up;" it incorporates the long-term development of the business.

Focusing on the Concept

During the initial phase of the planning process, the prospective entrepreneur should develop the first three parts of the business plan:
- Brief History of the Business Concept
- Mission Statement
- Goals and Objectives

Keeping the mission statement, goals, and objectives succinct and focused is of utmost importance. Paul Hawken, author of *Growing a Business*, states that a person should *"... reduce your business idea to its apparent essence. Then reduce it again. A nationwide chain must begin with the process of establishing a nearly microscopic kernel of what will become that national chain."* Although the concept is concise, the work of developing the business needs to be thorough and exacting. As Hawken says, *"Cutting the first corner is a beginning of a different sort – the beginning of failure."*[1]

When a feasible business idea is developed, the prospective entrepreneur needs to determine if the concept can be converted into a viable business. The mission statement, goals, and objectives will be the focus for developing the additional parts of the business plan, which are:

111

- Marketing Plan, including both market research and marketing
- Operations Plan, including basic activities of the business, human resources planning, and accommodations for disabilities
- Financial Plan, including the financial projects

As business planning takes shape, the goals may be modified to meet the needs of the market, the capabilities of the business, or initial financial limitations. The marketing, operations, and financial plans may need to be reassessed to ensure that they are directed toward meeting the modified business goals.

Although the written business plan has distinct sections, these functions intertwine with one another when the business is up and running. Creating business strategies and methods, as well as resolving problems and challenges, requires a global perspective on the business.

Therefore, rather than analyzing the business plan section by section, this chapter brings in the businessperson's perspectives on the challenges, strategies, and methods for creating a successful business. Since the challenges and strategies often have special implications for persons with disabilities, these aspects are addressed as an integral part of the business planning process.

Determining the Hurdles to Overcome

In *"Dimensions of Perceived Entrepreneurial Obstacles,"* author Patricia Greene, the Ewing Marion Kauffman/Missouri Chair in Entrepreneurial Leadership at the Henry W. Bloch School of Business and Public Administration (University of Missouri), describes the primary business obstacles as seen by entrepreneurs. Greene used responses from New Jersey small business owners participating in a survey conducted jointly by the Rutgers Center for Entrepreneurial Management and the Rutgers Small Business Development Center.[2]

The business owners ranked the obstacles that they encountered during the start-up of their businesses. I have added the business plan counterparts (marketing/finance/operation) to these rankings to show that the business plan sections underlie pragmatic challenges for the business.

- sales, especially the first customers - marketing/finance/operations
- start-up financing - finance
- managing cash flow - operations/finance
- attracting good employees - operations
- gaining relevant knowledge and skills - operations

The entrepreneurs also ranked the obstacles that they encountered at the time the survey was conducted, when their businesses were established.

- sales - marketing/finance
- competition - marketing
- keeping good employees - operations

- government paperwork/compliance - operations
- managing accounts receivable - operations/finance
- managing time - operations

Developing strategies and methods to overcome these challenges is essential to the success of the business. When the strategies and methods are well-designed in the business planning stage, operation of the business will go more smoothly and successfully. When they are not developed as part of the business design, pitfalls and problems occur that negatively impact the stability and profitability of the business.

The survey findings listed here are in agreement with my experience as a business consultant working with numerous small business clients. Entrepreneurs starting up businesses see the importance of financial capital, sales income, and (particularly as the business starts to grow) good employees. The importance of other "operations" aspects of the business, such as systems for financial management, employee retention, and time management, are not always of immediate interest. They may require a significant problem or challenge before they are addressed in depth.

The "operations" section of the business plan is extremely important, because it provides the business with a means to run the business in an integrated and continuous manner. When problems occur, as they will for all businesses, the operating procedures are a means of holding the business together, finding solutions to problems, and, in extreme cases, regrouping or reorganizing the business.

A primary business planning goal should be to anticipate and confront both start-up and future business challenges. The prospective business owner who addresses these challenges directly and assertively will most likely succeed in understanding and managing the proposed business.

While formulating methods to deal with business challenges, it is important to retain the perspective for entrepreneurs with disabilities. Urban Miyares, founder of the Disabled Businesspersons Association, states, " ... *most people, who are not familiar with working with the disabled, tend to be task-of-business focused, concentrating on what you need to do to make the business successful. But, with the disabled, you need to be people-oriented, clearly understanding the position, limitations, and abilities of the potential business owner, then figuring out what needs to be done to make the business successful, given these guidelines.*"[3]

A COMPANY MUST IDENTIFY, ATTRACT, AND RETAIN CUSTOMERS IN
ORDER TO HAVE THE NECESSARY INCOME TO KEEP THE BUSINESS
RUNNING ON A LONG-TERM BASIS.

Sales and Competition (Marketing and Finance)

Despite all the attention that surrounds obtaining start-up loans and investments, the chief source of business financing is revenue from sales. Successful marketing strategies produce sales that bring in the revenue to run the business and pay the entrepreneur's salary. A company must identify, attract, and retain customers in order to have the necessary income to keep the business running on a long-term basis.

Getting out into the world and finding customers, especially those first customers, is a major challenge for many small business owners. It can be intimidating, and the prospective entrepreneur may not know where to start. When a person has disabilities, the initial marketing steps can be even more challenging.

Sometimes a person's disabilities can make it hard to get to where the customers are, or make it difficult to communicate with the prospective customers. The person with disabilities may not have the necessary self-confidence, or may wonder how he or she will be received due to the disabilities. Marketing and sales take considerable energy, which also impacts many people with disabilities. Despite these additional challenges, people with disabilities do find effective methods for marketing their products or services.

Researching the Market

Since knowledge is power, a marketing effort includes research into the economy, the target industry, the prospective market for the product or service, competitors, and potential customers. Extensive research can be done on the Internet, at the library, and on the telephone. Although it may take a considerable amount of time to accumulate information and understand its importance and implications for a new business concept, there is less time pressure in this planning stage than after the business is up and running. This is also a good place to start testing one's personal abilities, disabilities, and stamina against the needs of the business.

Research on the general business environment and a specific industry should provide the entrepreneur with a perspective on how a new business venture might fit into that industry, find a niche in the market, and become a profitable venture. The niche market may be a geographic area, a certain type of customer, a product or service that has a unique characteristic, a method for delivery of the product or service, or other creative aspects designed to satisfy a potential group of customers. To fit a niche market, the business idea should be honed down and refined to the "kernel" to which Paul Hawkens referred.

RESEARCH SHOULD PROVIDE A PERSPECTIVE ON HOW A NEW BUSINESS VENTURE MIGHT FIT INTO AN INDUSTRY, FIND A NICHE IN THE MARKET, AND BECOME A PROFITABLE VENTURE.

Market research can be accomplished at a relatively low cost. Publications and Internet resources are a good starting point for finding general business information as well as data and resources on specific industries.

The Encyclopedia of Business Information Sources, published by Gale Research Inc., provides a list of titles on 1,100 business subjects, including "statistical sources, books, handbooks, manuals, trade associations, periodicals, financial ratios, almanacs and yearbooks, directories, price sources, abstract services and indices, and computer databases." University library web sites are an excellent resource to find additional sources for business information. Ohio University library has a very extensive web-site with business reference resources at: www.library.ohiou.edu/Subjects/business.htm.

As the market research effort progresses, it becomes more interactive. You might contact relevant trade associations, people who own businesses, people working in the same type or related businesses, and business counseling resources. Starting points for this type of research includes, but definitely are not limited to:

- the Small Business Administration, which has a web-site listing its local offices, Service Corp of Retired Executives (SCORE) offices, Small Business Development Centers (SBDC), Business Information Centers (BIC), Tribal BICs, and One-Stop Capital Shops: www.sba.gov
- trade associations, which can provide extensive information on specific industries
- government and business economic development organizations at the state, county, or city level. At the local level chambers of commerce are often a comfortable starting point.
- nonprofit organizations that assist in training or have micro-loan programs for prospective small businesses

A significant portion of this research can be accomplished by telephone. However, getting out and meeting with businesspeople is an essential aspect of business planning and development. Face-to-face meetings:

- improve communications with the economic and business resources, allowing more extensive interactions and more in-depth conversations
- allow the potential entrepreneur to visit other businesses, seeing in person how existing businesses function
- assist in establishing networking relationships and potential business arrangements

- enable entrepreneurs with disabilities to interact with the economic development and business community

Market research tools also include surveys and focus groups. However, these types of research should be conducted by market research professionals to ensure the validity of the results. Consequently, the price may be prohibitive for small start-up businesses.

Researching the Competition

If the market is local, investigating competition often can be done directly by the prospective entrepreneur. If the market is more expansive, other types of contact are necessary. With more businesses having Internet web-sites, checking out competitive web-sites can determine many of the major characteristics and pricing policies of the competition.

There are general aspects of competitive companies that affect most businesses, regardless of the industry. These aspects include:
- business location
- physical size of the business
- appearance of the business
- the types of surrounding businesses
- the demographics of the surrounding residential areas and retail locations
- types of customers attracted to the business
- variety and quality of the products and services
- marketing and sales materials, including types of media used
- sales methods
- pricing, sale, and discount policies
- estimated dollar volume for the business
- primary times for business traffic (retail locations)

Each type of business also will have unique competitive characteristics to research. Discussions with industry sources will point the direction toward understanding the unique characteristic for a particular industry. Additional competitive characteristics also may be uncovered in the process of doing the competitive research.

Pricing and Financial Research

When evaluating competitive pricing, look beyond the price. A product or service can provide unique qualities. For example, it might have exceptional durability or be sold by helpful sales people. You might offer a comfortable surrounding in which to shop, personalized service, a long-term warranty, ongoing service/support, effective delivery services, or other attributes that make it valuable to the customer. It is the value perceived by the customer that creates competitive pricing.

In order to understand pricing, it is necessary to know the underlying costs and profits for a specific industry. It is advantageous to analyze this information with the assistance of an accounting professional, who can put the information in practical terms for a potential business owner.

There are a number of resources for financial information covering a wide range of industries. These resources describe the ratios for various expenses and profits by industry and business size. *Industrial Norms and Key Business Ratios,* by Dun and Bradstreet, Inc., and *Robert Morris Associates Annual Statement Studies* by Robert Morris Associates are two of the principal references.

Other resources for general business and industry specific financial ratio and norms are available. The Long Business and Economics Library at the Haas School of Business at the University of California, Berkeley, lists many of these publications at its web site: www.lib.berkeley.edu/BUSI/bbg6.html.

Direct Customer Research

Eventually all businesses need to test their products or services on customers. This may be done by providing free or low cost demonstration products or services, with the provision that the user will provide feedback about the product or service. "Beta" versions of new software products or upgrades are classic examples of this type of research.

Sometimes a business finds customers willing to pay full price when the product or service is still in development, or is new to the market. These customers are valuable sources for feedback. (See "First Customers" box on page 18.) Hearing feedback from customers is an interactive, ongoing process for improving products and services, and adjusting to market changes.

Marketing and Sales

Some people love to market and sell their products and services. Other people want to have businesses, but they do not feel comfortable marketing and selling.

Thus there are two choices: at least one of the business owners must be willing and able to sell or an employee, broker, or sales representative must be found to do it. The second alternative might be more appealing to some people with disabilities, but it is not always financially possible to pay for direct sales costs when a business is first starting out.

Even if a company can afford to pay commissions or salaries, the brokers, sales representatives, or employees will not maintain a continuing relationship with the company if the products or services do not sell readily. The Internet is another inviting non-personal alternative. However, effective

First Customers

Making the first sales to customers is a significant step. The initial sales serve as part of the research process as well as the beginning of the marketing and sales process. This is a starting point for understanding how best to serve the market though dialogue with customers.

First sales:

- show that the products or services are salable
- boost the entrepreneur's confidence and enthusiasm for the business
- teach methods for selling the products or services that can be duplicated, improved, and expanded upon
- offer customers an opportunity to provide feedback on the products or service, describing how it fit their needs, changes or additions that they would like to see, and the pricing that they feel is appropriate. This is the beginning of a communications cycle with customers focused on continually improving the quality of the company's products and services. This communication also helps entrepreneurs stay at the forefront of trends and changes in the market.
- give customers a chance to work directly with the entrepreneur on testing and developing the product or service
- let customers serve as references for sales to other potential customers if they find the products or services beneficial
- let satisfied customers recommend other potential buyers to do business with the company

Internet sales can be extremely expensive to achieve. Usually, the Internet is a supplementary sales method, even for large, well-known companies.

For those business owners who have not had an interest or experience in marketing, there are ways to become more marketing- and sales-oriented. I believe that the most important step in marketing is to truly believe in what is being sold and to believe that it will improve the lives or businesses of the people to whom it is sold.

It is difficult to continually sell a product or service without this attitude. Therefore, an important part of the marketing effort is the development of goods or services that have positive attributes and qualities for their market.

To actually approach people face-to-face is an obstacle for some individuals, especially those people who have not had the opportunity to sell or work with customers before starting their own business. This is a skill that can be learned.

At the lower cost end of the spectrum, Toastmaster International (a nonprofit organization) teaches *"better listening, thinking, and speaking."*

THE MOST IMPORTANT STEP IN MARKETING IS TO TRULY BELIEVE IN WHAT IS BEING SOLD AND TO BELIEVE THAT IT WILL IMPROVE THE LIVES OR BUSINESSES OF THE PEOPLE TO WHOM IT IS SOLD.

The Toastmaster goal is to help people lose their fear of public speaking and improve skills in communications, whether speaking before a group, leading a team, or conducting a meeting. With 8,500 clubs worldwide, groups can be found in most urban and rural areas. The Toastmaster web-site is: www.toastmasters.org.

There are also classes in public speaking and dramatic arts at community colleges. A more expensive resource is the Dale Carnegie Training courses. Dale Carnegie has been in business for fifty years, training people in a range of communications skills, including sales training. The web-site at www.dale-carnegie.com provides access to their substantial listing of classes, their location in large and moderate-sized urban areas, and useful tips on ways to improve communication and presentation skills.

Marketing practices develop over the life of the business. Books and tapes on marketing and sales, seminars on sales, and sales training programs are available to enhance a company's abilities to sell its products or services. The key is to find the methods that best fit the business, and are priced reasonably considering the financial resources of the company.

Start-Up Financing (Finance)

Start-up financing is a challenge but it is should not be a roadblock. The bad news is that unless a businessperson puts up personal collateral, such as a home or investments, a commercial bank is unlikely to loan money to a start-up business. Most speculative investors will not either, since they require a high probability for a substantial return on their investment.

In 1996 *Inc. Magazine* interviewed the CEOs of their "500 fastest growing companies" to determine how they found their start-up capital. Sixty-two percent of the companies financed the business from their personal savings, mortgaged property, or used their credit cards. Another 13% obtained financing from family or friends. Business partners and other employees accounted for another 8%. Venture capitalist and "angel" investors were only 6%. Bank loans accounted for just 2%.[4]

Now the good news. Many businesses can be started relatively inexpensively, as the Montana/Wyoming Job Training Partnership Program illustrates in Chapter 7. There are resources for people with disabilities for business training, skills training, disability-related equipment, business assets, and business expenses.[5]

Although there still are only a few micro-loan programs directed specifically for people with disabilities, micro-loan programs in general have expanded exponentially. The National Community Capital Association, a non-profit organization of micro-lenders, reports that in 1985 they collectively managed $28 million in loans, which increased to $800 million in 1999.[6] Many entrepreneurs with disabilities have access to these programs, which assist prospective business owners who cannot obtain conventional financing.

In preparation to obtain financing, start with a focused business idea, develop a viable business plan, determine how to manage the business economically and prudently, and use creative thinking and analytical reasoning rather than dollars to resolve issues whenever possible. If these objectives are reached, it is likely that the necessary investments, loans, or funding will be available.

Managing Cash Flow/Accounts Receivable (Operations/Finance)

In its simplest terms, cash flow analysis is determining when money comes into the business and when it goes out in payments. Managing cash flow is important for all small business owners, but it is critical for many entrepreneurs with disabilities who frequently are living financially "on the edge" when starting up their businesses. If incoming payments to the company do not arrive in time to cover the current business expenses, the business owner is in a financial bind. He or she may need to deplete personal funds, normally used for necessary living expenses, in order to keep the business solvent.

There are three major factors involving cash flow:
- getting customers to pay the business on time
- making payment to vendors on a timely basis
- coordinating the cash flow process, so that the business runs smoothly

Getting Customers to Pay on Time

The businesses that receive most of their payments when the product or service is delivered have little problem getting customers to pay. The businesses that provide credit for their customers have more of a challenge collecting money in a timely manner.

The first step is for the company to set up a billing system and institute consistent billing practices, including invoices or billing statements that clearly state when the payment is due. Some companies offer a range of pay-

> ## Record-Keeping and Financial Management
> The first rule to follow in business financial management is to keep records for the business separate from personal records. At a minimum the business should have its own checking account, savings, or money market account and its own credit card. If an expense is paid for personally, the business should reimburse the expense, using a receipt to verify the purchase.
>
> If a PASS plan is part of the business financial strategy, there is an additional level of record-keeping. Without this separation of financial records, the entrepreneur is vulnerable to significant fines and penalties, which even could cause the company to close down. Additionally, the auditing entity will require the time-consuming, and potentially costly, process of correcting the records.

ment terms for different types of customers. This includes varying payment due dates, different discount amounts, or varying payment dates for discounts.

You may do this to meet the needs of certain types of customers, such as selling to wholesale customers vs. retail customers. Or, it may be to gain the business of specific customers, for instance a large purchaser. Well-designed computer accounting systems, even those available at a modest price, can allow for these variable terms and predict the timing for the company's cash inflow.

Difficulties crop up when customers do not pay on time, especially ones owing substantial balances. The company will need to have cash on hand to pay its own bills while it is waiting for these delinquent customers to pay their account balances.

Active steps should be taken to collect from delinquent customers when it is apparent that the accounts are overdue. You can follow up with the customer in writing, talk directly to the person who can facilitate payment, or work out an extended payment schedule. There are alternative methods for recovering delinquent payments if these straightforward methods fail, but these should be used with discretion since they take money directly from the company's profits.

A *line of credit* from a financial institution allows a company to borrow when its cash is low and pay down the loan as the income comes in. Although the line of credit is available all year, the company is charged interest only when there is actual borrowing. Usually the line of credit must be paid off completely for a specific number of days each year.

"Factors" are businesspeople who buy a company's accounts receivables. They pay the company for the receivables immediately, but their fee for this service comes to a significant percentage of the amount due on the receivable.

TAKE ACTIVE STEPS TO COLLECT FROM DELINQUENT CUSTOMERS WHEN IT IS APPARENT THAT THE ACCOUNTS ARE OVERDUE.

There also are collection agencies who may be able to collect part or all of the delinquent accounts. The company does not receive any cash until the money is collected from the delinquent customer. The agencies receive a percentage of the amount that they are able to collect from the customer. Their fees are less than those taken by the factors, but they cannot guarantee collection.

Few companies are free from some late paying or delinquent customers. To minimize the risk of taking on customers who may be delinquent or may default on payments, prospective customers can be required to fill out credit applications including credit references, pay cash on delivery (COD), make a partial payment before the product is ordered, or pay a retainer before services are provided.

Making Payments to Vendors on a Timely Basis

This portion of the cash flow equation requires paying vendors in a systematic and consistent manner. At a basic level, this will include tracking when regular or monthly bills are due, noting when large payments are due, and determining specific dates during the month to designate for paying bills. Vendor payment terms need to be taken into consideration.

Payment terms vary between industries, and from company to company. For example, one industry practice may be to provide terms for extending payment, perhaps up to ninety days. Another industry might require a prepayment or cash on delivery. Many vendors provide discounts to encourage prompt payment, allowing the purchaser to accrue significant savings over time. Well-designed computer accounting software assists in keeping vendor payments on time and in taking advantage of vendor discounts.

Some companies choose to pay their vendors slowly when they are low on cash. This is an unwise practice that can cause serious long-term problems. It can harm the relationship with the vendors, who may play an important role in the growth of a small business. A positive strategy is to pay small, local vendors particularly quickly. It is a way of saying "thank you" for continually providing reliable products and services.

Coordinating the Cash Flow Process

The "art" of cash flow management is coordinating incoming payments with the outflow of cash. Unfortunately, the company sales, the incoming payments, and the outgoing expenses often do not line up in a neat row. Running out of money, whether on the short term or long term, can be a devastating circumstance.

PAY SMALL, LOCAL VENDORS PARTICULARLY QUICKLY. IT IS A WAY OF SAYING "THANK YOU" FOR CONTINUALLY PROVIDING RELIABLE PRODUCTS AND SERVICES.

Setting up an easy-to-follow cash flow spreadsheet as part of the company accounting system can greatly ease cash flow management. Basic financial systems include budgeting; a bookkeeping system producing monthly financial statements; and daily, weekly, or semimonthly cash flow analysis (depending on the type of business).

These are not difficult systems to establish, but they do require oversight by an experienced bookkeeper or CPA. Additional financial spreadsheets and accounting system applications evolve as the company grows, assisting the entrepreneur in retaining control of the financial aspects of the business.

Attracting and Keeping Good Employees (Operation)

The first steps in creating and maintaining an effective workforce are:
- determining the type of work that could be accomplished by employees, such as production, sales, office, delivery
- defining the work that would be accomplished by each of the employees
- determining the cost of the employees, including federal, state, and local payroll taxes, federal and state unemployment insurance, workers' compensation, employee benefits, and any other related cost (which can vary with the state, county or city)
- analyzing the employee cost as part of the income and expense budget
- deciding when the business can afford to hire each employee, whether part-time or full-time

Finding Employees

There are no easy answers for finding good employees. Finding employees who will fit the needs of the business usually starts with clearly defining the jobs that they will perform. Job descriptions should include the essential components of the position and the requirements for the applicants, including education and experience. They can include other aspects of the job, for example, the number of hours, days and times to work, strength requirement, and licensing. The more defined the job description, the more likely that the communication with prospective employees will be clear and effective.

There are a variety of ways to find employees. The least expensive, and sometimes the most successful method, is by word of mouth to people in the same or related industries.

Some entrepreneurs with disabilities, especially those who were consumers of state vocational rehabilitation (VR) programs, use VR as a resource for finding qualified employees. There is the potential for tax credits for the company, assistance with work-related accommodations, and job training or coaching for the worker with disabilities. There is no charge for this service. State employment offices provide another means of finding employees without a fee for either the employer or the employee.

Advertising for employees can be inexpensive, though large or display ads can become costly. When you place classified ads for employees, it is important to find publications that will reach the right people. Publications include suburban or neighborhood papers, city or county-wide papers, or trade magazines.

Using employment agencies or employee search firms can be expensive for start-up businesses. Understanding the fee system is essential before working with these agencies.

You should not rush the hiring process. Resumes are the first level of applicant screening. Interview a job applicant more than one time and by more than one person within the company, possibly even by knowledgeable people outside of company. This type of thorough interviewing process is particularly important for a prospective employee who will play a key role in the company. Calling prior employment references is helpful. However, companies often feel constrained about conveying negative information regarding a previous employee. Lawful, thoughtful, and thorough hiring procedures should improve the prospect of employing workers whose capabilities mesh with the needs of the business and who fit into the company's culture.

Employees as Accommodations for Entrepreneurs with Disabilities

An entrepreneur with disabilities may need either full- or part-time employee(s) to assist with work that is difficult or impossible due to the owner's disabilities. Although paying additional wages makes the business more expensive to run, the work these employees do is often a necessary factor for the success of the business. These employees provide the needed skills that allow an entrepreneur with disabilities to run a competitive business.

Small Business Employment Strategies

Small businesses have some advantages as employers since there are many people who would rather work for a small business than for a corporate giant. Small business owners usually know all of their employees and work directly with them to some extent.

When small business owners see an employee working out well for the company, they can provide a salary increase, incentives, learning resources, and "business tools" without having to take the time and effort to go through a bureaucracy. Small companies can provide "cross-training" on jobs, enabling the employee to learn more skills while giving the company a more flexible workforce.

The owners also can provide flexibility in hours (within some limitations set by federal and state overtime laws) and perhaps flexibility in workplace. Although these strategies are used to varying degrees by large corporations, small business owners are in a unique position to be responsive to the needs and abilities of their individual employees. Most entrepreneurs with disabilities will have looked long and hard at accommodations for their abilities and disabilities. They can use this same perspective to be supportive of workers both with and without disabilities.

Business owners need to know competitive salaries in order to get and keep good employees. Discussions with other business owners and information from trade associations should aid in determining salaries. Additional strategies include talking to recruiting companies and temporary employment agencies (regarding the salaries that they pay, not the hourly charges to their customers), and keeping an eye on classified advertisements in local newspapers.

A small, start-up business may find it difficult to pay competitive salaries. However, there are other ways to meet the needs and desires of employees. Small business owners might allow employees to work more autonomously, move up faster professionally, have their ability and creativity acknowledged, have a definable career path, experience a supportive group atmosphere, truly be a part of a team, work on more selective projects or products, or work for a company less prone to mergers. Companies can give out bonuses in good years as a method of compensating people for working for a lower base salary. The bonus also encourages employees to work toward the company goals and profitability.

Although benefits programs are often relatively more expensive for small companies, some company benefits are cost effective. "Cafeteria plans" (covering healthcare, dependent care, and payment for insurance coverage) only have a small administrative cost to the company, while allowing employees to spend pre-tax dollars in these areas.

There are retirement programs with low administrative costs, and matching company contributions can be optional. A number of other benefits are listed in the Chapter 5. Benefits that are positive factors for the business owner with disabilities are likely to be positive for the other company employees.

Employees are a significant factor in the company's reaching its business goals and achieving its mission. It is important to keep employees informed about the business, so that they understand what they are able to achieve for the company and for themselves. A small business can have regular staff meetings that include all, or at least most, of the employees.

Annual company retreats also provide a means for informing and listening to employees. In a small company, the owner can communicate directly with all of the employees. The owner can understand what motivates an individual employee, beyond salary, and find individual methods to reward actions that support the goals of the business.

Regardless of how the company treats its employees, some people will resign from the company. Additionally, the company may need to terminate one or more of its workers. The company should be structured to minimize adverse effects that can occur when an employee leaves a small business. The employee's work should be transferable to an existing or a new employee. This might require documentation of the job functions or cross-training with other employees. Critical or complex job functions should be assigned to workers who are likely to be long-term employees. To have a secure future for the business, you should have a plan for how the company will continue if a key employee leaves.

Gaining Relevant Knowledge and Skills (Operations)

Gaining relevant knowledge and skills applies both to successfully running a business and to creating the products or services produced by the business. This is a place where some people with disabilities may get a leg up. In the Montana/Wyoming Job Training Partnership Program, for example, most of the prospective business owners were able to obtain entrepreneurial skills training, occupational skills training, or job coaching. Training was equally available for conventional employment and self-employment, since training is a mandate for vocational rehabilitation and the other job training programs.[7]

Training is an ongoing process for most entrepreneurs. Finding the time and budgeting the money is an essential part of running the business in the long term. Sometimes seminars and educational programs are required to keep up in a field. In other instances books, periodicals, and informal meetings with people in the field can provide the learning necessary to stay current and get ahead in a particular line of business.

It is important to determine if certificates or licenses are required for the company or its employees. Sometimes they are not required, but the training involved in obtaining them can improve the employees' skills. Certification and licensing gives customers more confidence in the company's and the employees' capabilities.

Learning should not be limited to the entrepreneur; it should spread throughout the company. A wide range of knowledge shared by many employees expands the capabilities of the entire organization. Educational opportunities also are a benefit for those employees who are motivated to expand their skills.

Government Paper Work/Compliance (Operations)

All companies have some level of government reporting, starting with sales tax, use tax, and personal or corporate income tax. Once a company has an employee, there are government payroll taxes, unemployment insurance, and workers' compensation insurance. When companies sell products or services to the government or are involved in businesses with government regulations, record-keeping and compliance can take a considerable amount of time and energy. It is important not to have this record-keeping take the focus of the owners and the employees away from the primary goals of the business.

Government reports must be kept up to date and sent in on a timely basis. Additionally, any company can be audited! These audits go faster and more successfully if the accounting and record keeping is done in a professional and consistent manner, with records kept in an orderly and easy to follow system, and forms filled out in line with requirements.

An employee who is planning to work long-term for the company should be trained and knowledgeable in this area or the work should be contracted out to people who specialize in this function. For example, payroll services are affordable for most businesses and can save companies from costly mistakes.

Entrepreneurs with disabilities who use PASS plans for their businesses will have an additional form of government record-keeping and reporting.

Having professional guidance in this area can prove prudent. Whether the record-keeping and reporting is handled from within the company or is contracted out, the cost of doing it correctly the first time is usually far more economical and time efficient than being "caught" by the government in even one mistake.

Managing Time (Operations)

Managing time is a challenge for all business owners, but people with disabilities also need to incorporate the time required by their disabilities into their day. The cost of not taking the necessary time to take care of and accommodate disabilities can be detrimental, even leading to increased disability. Business owners with disabilities will find taking care of themselves essential, so that they can work relatively comfortably and effectively, while retaining functionality and health.

Matters related to disabilities must be part of the schedule for the day, integrated into the work schedule. Some disabilities affect the time and energy it takes to bathe, dress, eat, and otherwise be able to function on a daily basis. Reasonable time must be allotted to these activities, or the entrepreneur will find the work schedule rushed and overloaded. Conforming to medication schedules and other regularly required medical needs can also affect the flow of the day's activities.

Some disabilities require less structured activities, such as physical therapy, diet, and rest. These are easier to dismiss, because they may not cause immediate problems. However, over the long term, omissions can adversely effect the entrepreneur's disabilities. If these activities are not included at least informally in the schedule, there eventually will be a detrimental effect.

Having disabilities makes it even more essential to determine the amount of time and energy required to do all of the job functions of the business owner. This determination should include the type of assistance needed to accomplish the job functions effectively. If the entrepreneur with disabilities does not keep the hours worked and the energy expended on the business within control, the fatigue and stress can fuel adverse effects on the disabilities.

These recommendations sound like common sense, but they are ongoing challenges for people with disabilities. Entrepreneurs with disabilities often feel pressure to do more work than is realistic in order to compete in the world. It is easy for them to get overcommitted or to allow disability needs to fall to the wayside in the exhilaration of creating, managing, and growing a business. Even more than business owners without disabilities, entrepreneurs with disabilities must focus their energy in the areas where they are most productive for their businesses.

Positive Aspects of Disability Work-Arounds

Urban Miyares, founder of the Disabled Businesspersons Association, sums up the perspective of the entrepreneur with disabilities: "An entrepreneur with disabilities needs the same qualities as a non-disabled business owner, plus the disabled person must develop a strategy to work around his or her disability."[8]

A creative entrepreneurial challenge for business owners with disabilities is developing strategies to work around disabilities in a manner that also creates positive benefits for their customers. There are entrepreneurs with disabilities who invent, manufacture, or sell products that assist them in living with their own disabilities. Their customers have products designed, produced, or sold by a person who lives with and truly understands the benefits and uses for the product.

In *Unlikely Entrepreneurs,* author RoseAnne Herzog profiles a successful entrepreneur who is profoundly deaf. One of his strategies for dealing with his communication disability is to provide such excellent and speedy service that his customers rarely need to talk to him.[9]

A cleaning service owner with a visual impairment uses her sense of touch to overcome her visual limitations. She provides her customers with superior service by tactilely finding and cleaning tiny bits of food and dirt on counters and tables that a person could miss visually.

As a consultant to human services organizations on "Entrepreneurship for People with Disabilities," I bring my clients sixteen years of experience as a businessowner coping with disabilities in addition to my professional business consulting background. My extensive personal experience researching and developing ways to succeed in my own businesses provides my clients with insights into the long-term challenges for entrepreneurs with disabilities, and methods for business owners to overcome limitations caused by their disabilities.

Like businesspeople everywhere, entrepreneurs with disabilities succeed by focusing on their abilities, not their limitations. Entrepreneurs with disabilities learn to use their abilities to overcome disability-related challenges, while improving the quality of their products and services for their customers.

LIKE BUSINESSPEOPLE EVERYWHERE, ENTREPRENEURS WITH DISABILITIES SUCCEED BY FOCUSING ON THEIR ABILITIES, NOT THEIR LIMITATIONS.

Sources:
1. Hawken, Paul, (1988). *The Companion Volume to Growing a Business: The 17-part PBS Series*. New York, NY: Fireside by Simon and Schuster.
2. Greene, Patricia G., University of Missouri, (1998). "Dimensions of Perceived Entrepreneurial Obstacles," Babson College/Arthur M. Blank Center for Entrepreneurship, web-site: www.babson.edu/entrep/fer/papers98/II/II_B/II_B_text.htm.
3. Miyares, Urban, (1996). Personal Communication Regarding the Development of the Colorado Division of Vocational Rehabilitation Self-Employment Program.
4. (1996). "Inc. Magazine 500," *Inc. Magazine.*
5. Shelley, Roger, Hayes, Tom, Newman, Lisa, and Griffin, Cary, (1999). "A New Formula for Success in Montana: Choice + Flexibility," *Bringing Home the Bacon, Inventive Self-Employment & Supported Employment in Rural America.* Missoula: Rural Institute/University of Montana.
6. (1999). Making Money Work for the Community, brochure for the 15th Annual Training Conference, National Community Capital Association web-site: www.communitycapital.org.
7. Shelley, Roger, Hayes, Tom, Newman, Lisa, and Griffin, Cary, (1999). "A New Formula for Success in Montana: Choice + Flexibility," *Bringing Home the Bacon, Inventive Self-Employment & Supported Employment in Rural America.* Missoula: Rural Institute/University of Montana.
8. Miyares, Urban, (1996). "Qualifications," *Starting/Expanding a Small Business*, Bold Business Consultants web-site: www.effectivecompensation.com/bold-owners.
9. Herzog, RoseAnne, (1998). *Unlikely Entrepreneurs: A Business Start-Up Guide for People with Disabilities and Chronic Health Conditions*, Traverse City, MI: North Peak Publishing.

CASE STUDY IV:
Corey's Electronic Bargains
Business Plan Summary

The business, Corey's Electronic Bargains, will be owned and operated by myself, Corey Huff of Berryville, Arkansas. The business will be primarily a consignment shop with additional items being placed for sale by myself as I deem necessary. Items carried by the store will include: video games, televisions, stereos, and computers. I will advertise for one month previous to the store opening in order to gain items. I also will purchase a certain amount of merchandise myself to ensure that the store will be fully stocked. Upon the store's opening, sales will be based on a 50/50 consignment rate, meaning that for every item sold, I will retain 50% of the value. The value of items that I purchase for sale will be retained 100%.

There are three key reasons behind starting a consignment business. First, many people in this area live on fixed or low incomes and cannot afford higher-priced merchandise from major retail stores. They also will have a venue to sell items in a retail environment for extra income. Second, competition is limited, as the two other consignment shops in the area are more oriented to clothing. Third, individuals entering into a consignment contract with Corey's Electronic Bargains would receive more of the item's value than if they went to a pawn shop, which only gives 20% of the book value of items.

On a personnel level, I have been advised to start a business that was home-based and computer-oriented. This did not suit my personality as I am an outgoing individual who seeks interaction with others more often than what a computer business might provide. Buying and selling items at flea markets and garage sales has been my hobby. Therefore, in operating a consignment store, I would be doing something I love on a daily basis. It would allow me to be out in the community, and I would be providing a necessary outlet for community members to buy and sell electronic items.

Advertising
I will place an advertisement in the local newspaper, *The Trader*, for approximately one month prior to the store's opening. The advertisement will ask for electronic items in good working order. I will determine the condition of the referred items and will provide a contract outlining the consignment agreement.

Ongoing advertisement will follow as deemed necessary, according to stock levels. In addition the storefront will have a professional sign that is eye-catching. This will attract customers, as the store itself will be located on the square in Berryville, Arkansas.

Competition

Competition is limited. Two stores in the immediate area are also consignment shops, but they concentrate on clothing sales. Therefore, I will be offering goods that are not offered by anyone else except for major retailers. Corey's Electronic Bargains will offer similar items at lower prices. If the need for other types of items is encountered, I reserve the right to add those items to remain competitive, increasing sales and potentially expanding the business.

Support

I require staff to assist me in my daily living. In devising this business and its plan, there was collaboration with my case manager in order to secure supported employment services during the hours that the business will be open. We also are approaching the Area Agency on Aging to find potential store "helpers" who would prefer to be out in the community rather than going to an activity center. The issue of supports is not a serious concern, as there are many outlets and individuals willing and ready to assist me in my store.

Store Hours

Tuesday - Friday	9:30 am to 6:00 pm
Saturday	9:30 am to 6:00 pm
Sunday	12:00 pm to 4:00 pm

Corey's Electronic Bargains will have extended hours on the weekend because more people are off from work and there is more traffic through Berryville at those times. Monday will be my day off. Store hours will be as stated unless the customer base expresses the need for different times and/or days.

Start-Up Costs

First six months' rent	$1,500
Utility hook-ups	370
First three months' utilities	420
Licenses	60
Bank accounts (two, including one for consignments)	100
Printed contracts	90
Ledgers and price tags	40
Insurance ($100,000 per year coverage)	350
Merchandise for start-up	800
Advertising	700
Business sign	200
Miscellaneous	370
TOTAL	$5,000

Business Loan

A business loan for $5,000 was made to Corey's Electronic Bargains through the Arkansas Support Network, Inc., through the Self-Employment Loan Fund. The Self-Employment Loan Fund makes loans to qualified applicants with disabilities and was made possible by a grant from the Arkansas Governor's Developmental Disabilities Council. The fund was developed through a partnership between Arkansas Support Network, Inc., and the National Center on Employment and Disability at the University of Arkansas.

This is a revolving loan with a self-replenishing fund. Currently the maximum loan is $5,000. Thus far the loan program has been funded by three grants from the Arkansas Governor's Development Disability Council. Applicants must first apply to the bank of their choice and be rejected for business loan in order to be considered. Once a person is accepted, project staff provide direction and guidance if the applicant requests assistance with investigation of possible business ventures or developing a business plan.

Some examples of loans made to businesses owned by persons with disabilities are below:

- Vending Machine Business: $5,000 for expansion of an existing business
- Web-site Designer: $5,000 loan to a home-based, start-up business to purchase a computer system (which was further modified by Arkansas Rehabilitation Services) and to pay for advertising
- Legal Abstracting Business: $5,000 to start a home-based business to pay for computer equipment, office furniture, postage, advertising, and some of the general operating expenses

After Opening: Views on Running a Retail Business

I enjoy running the business, although there are frustrations. Business is still sporadic, as we have been open only nine months. It took me some time to get a solid inventory of consignment and resale goods built up.

Store days are currently Tuesday through Friday. Weekends proved to be too slow at this time to warrant the store's being open. I am considering opening the store on Mondays to see if there is enough business to justify being open then.

I receive assistance with the store from my personal care attendant. She provides enough support for now, until business gets busier. My emphasis now is on finding ways to increase business, and I will determine my employee needs later on.

There are more men who are customers than women. Although electronics sell the best, I am bringing in more of a variety of small items that could attract more women, such as earrings. I am gradually starting to get repeat customers.

The business does not cover all of my expenses as yet. For the first six months the rent payments were covered by the loan. Now that I must pay the rent out of store revenues, I have had to put personal money into the business to meet expenses and loan payments. This is difficult, because my only other sources of income are Social Security and Medicaid. It is now early March, when retail trade is often slow. I am hopeful that sales will increase in the coming months. I am determined to succeed. I am willing to do all that I can to make the store succeed.

I used to go to yard sales as a hobby. I would buy items, then sell them at my own yard sale for double the price. When I found exceptional buys, I would make an even higher profit. This taught me about buying, selling, and pricing. However, it did not teach me the basics of business. I am going to take business courses at a nearby junior college to understand the basics of business management and more effective ways to run my business.

Several businesspeople in the community assist me with my business challenges, including the man from whom I rent store space. My parents both had small businesses, a janitorial business and an owner-operator trucking business. At first they were uncertain if I should take the risk of opening a business, but now they are supportive of my efforts.

My advice to other people with disabilities who are considering self-employment is to take your time! Do not rush into it. Learn as much as you can about the business. Research what is needed in your area. Determine what kind of business would make money.

Location is the most important factor. Find a location with the types of neighboring businesses that would encourage people to shop at your store. Having convenient and adequate parking is a necessary condition for a successful retail business.

Look carefully at how much money you will need. Then be prepared for hard times by putting away money both for the business and for personal needs.

Take business courses before starting the business. This will help to keep you from having to learn so much the hard way. Get assistance from other businesspeople in the community so that when you have questions or problems, you have people with experience to call upon.

Olivia Harrison, coordinator of housing and special projects for the Arkansas Support Network, Inc., assisted with business planning and start-up, and continues to provide business guidance and support to Corey's Electronic Bargains. Material for this case study has been taken from the Corey's Electronic Bargains business plan and an interview with Corey Huff. The business plan material has been edited to fit the format of this book; consequently, it does not contain all of the information that was in the original business plan. Most notably, financial planning and projects are not included.

Chapter 9
Designing Programs to Support Entrepreneurs with Disabilities

Human services and government organizations are a potentially rich resource for expanding the opportunities for entrepreneurship for people with disabilities. Many human services and government organizations have already participated in supporting self-employment as a means for people with disabilities to become productive members of the workforce. By 1999 the federal government showed increased activity in this area through the Small Business Administration (SBA), Treasury Department, President's Committee on Employment of People with Disabilities, and Job Accommodation Network (JAN).

Organizations can increase the potential for long-term, successful self-employment for people with disabilities by:

- making self-employment a viable employment choice for people with disabilities
- providing consumers who are interested in self-employment the opportunity to determine for themselves if they can create a feasible business concept and business plan
- creating self-employment programs to provide the support, guidance, training, and resources that enable entrepreneurs with disabilities to create workable business concepts and successful businesses

Self-Employment Programs Must Reflect the Organization and Its Consumers

Each self-employment program for people with disabilities will have its own distinct characteristics, reflecting the mission and goals for the organization creating the program. A self-employment program also should reflect:

- the level of commitment of the board, administration, and staff to self-employment as a viable employment choice for people with disabilities

- the characteristics and needs of the people served by the organization
- the skills, experiences, and attitudes of the human services workers and volunteers who will actively participate in the self-employment program
- the number of employee and volunteer hours that are available to the program
- the availability of other relevant internal resources, including work space, computers, staff training, and community coordinators
- the level of funding available and obtainable to support a self-employment program for entrepreneurs with disabilities
- the community business and economic resources with whom the organization is able and willing to collaborate

Due to these variables, each entrepreneurship program will be unique. There is no single prototype for self-employment programs for people with disabilities. Even when organizations are quite similar in their mission and goals for the organization, such as state vocational rehabilitation programs, the remaining variables come into play to create the program. For long-term success, each organization must address these variables.

Commitment: Key to a Successful Self-Employment Program

Perhaps the most crucial variable for a successful self-employment program is the level of commitment of the board, the administration, and the human services staff to self-employment as a viable employment choice for people with disabilities. Optimizing organizational commitment is one of the compelling reasons for customizing a program for an organization.

It may appear easier to bring in a "boiler-plate" program design or to adopt a design that was created by another agency. The program plan may be accepted and instituted because it takes much less effort to approve an existing model than to create a customized program. However, this process rarely creates the level of commitment needed for the long-term success of an innovative and dynamic program.

To have a strong and continuing level of commitment to a self-employment program, those persons who participate in the design and development of the program must feel that they are creating the best possible program for their organization and the people they serve. The individuals designing and developing the program must have the opportunity to:

- hear and see a full range of information on self-employment programs, to ascertain which methods are best for their organization

- make recommendations or express concerns, based on their knowledge of the organization and its consumers
- thoroughly question assumptions and processes of the program's design and its implementation
- debate these assumptions and processes with people who may have opposing views or concerns
- create a program that serves the unique capabilities and needs of the organization and its clientele
- comprehend the individual aspects of the program, and understand their relationship with one another

Consequently, those individuals will have the opportunity to create a self-employment program that is in the best interest of both their organization and their consumers. When this goal is accomplished, they will be able to:

- give the program their full acceptance and commitment
- gain a passion for the program, which enhances its probability for success
- work toward the success of the program that they were instrumental in developing
- willingly advocate for the program to other staff members, consumers, and community business and economic resources

Commitment at the Colorado Division of Vocational Rehabilitation

As the consultant and project leader for the Colorado Division of Vocational Rehabilitation (CDVR) Self-Employment Program Task Force, I saw how effective this strategy is for an organization. Prior to the creation of the Self-Employment Program Task Force, there were negative perceptions and grave concerns throughout CDVR regarding a self-employment program.

Despite this negativity, an entrepreneurship program was being considered seriously because a few people within CDVR knew it was time to implement an effective entrepreneurship program. At the same time, people with disabilities in the community were advocating for an entrepreneurship program and CDVR consumers were beginning to ask for self-employment as an employment choice. CDVR rehabilitation counselors began to look for ways to work effectively with job seekers who were asking about or insisting on self-employment.

The goal of the Self-Employment Program Task Force was to design an entrepreneurship program for CDVR that would:
- make self-employment an open and viable option for CDVR consumers
- have the support of CDVR's vocational rehabilitation administrators, supervisors, counselors, and support staff
- fit within the guidelines set by Rehabilitation Services Administration, the federal agency that oversees the state vocational rehabilitation programs

Diana Huerta, director of CDVR, selected the task force members, which included management level personnel, rehabilitation counselors, and support staff members. Prior to the start of the task force, I conducted several presentations with question-and-answer sessions for CDVR rehabilitation counselors, supervisors, support staff, and administrators. Most of the CDVR employees whom the director chose for the task force had participated in one or more of these pre-task force presentations. By the time the task force meetings began, its members were ready to listen to information on self-employment programs and to debate their views fully and aggressively.

The task force members' views encompassed a wide range of concerns and fears regarding the implementation of a self-employment program for people with disabilities. There had been many unsuccessful experiences with self-employment at CDVR in the past. However, a primary objective of the Self-Employment Program Task Force was to design a self-employment program that would overcome these previous problems by providing:
- the structure for an agency policy that would give rehabilitation counselors a mandate and direction regarding self-employment
- a well-designed, structured self-employment program
- the method for developing training for rehabilitation counselors, supervisors, and support staff on implementing the self-employment program for CDVR consumers
- the method for increased contact and relationships with business and economic development resources, which would work collaboratively with the self-employment program

At the completion of the design process, task force members had developed a self-employment program that they all could support despite their differing views concerned self-employment for people with disabilities. The members of the task force then made a strong commitment to the success of the program and communicated their support of it to their co-workers.

After the task force finished its work, all members worked actively on the development and implementation of the self-employment program. This was a voluntary effort. They responded in this positive manner despite having busy schedules, and began outreach to community economic and business resources.

The majority of the recommendations from the task force were accepted by the administrators immediately, giving the program a firm foundation. Training for rehabilitation counselors and supervisors began a few months later. Additional task force recommendations were incorporated into the program over the next two years, during which time there was additional staff training. The program has gained acceptance with the majority of CDVR counselors, particularly in urban areas, and the program is successfully serving an increasing number of CDVR consumers.

The program is not as strongly accepted by rural rehabilitation counselors. CDVR felt that there was an immediate need to get the program into rural areas, eliminating the recommended research and evaluation of rural self-employment issues. Consequently, rural counselors were not brought in to assist in designing the rural aspects of the program and the differing situations and needs of the rural CDVR consumers were not taken into consideration.

The lesson learned from this experience is that human services organizations and their customers are best served by taking the extra time and energy to include the rehabilitation counselors who serve people from diverse areas or with diverse characteristics, in the appropriate phase of the design process. Also, it is as important to carefully analyze the needs of rural self-employment consumers as it is to analyze their urban counterparts. This process will help to ensure that a self-employment program will have the support and acceptance of both urban and rural counselors, and that the needs of both urban and rural individuals are met in a logical and satisfactory manner.

Designing an Entrepreneurship Program for People with Disabilities

Entrepreneurship programs for people with disabilities need to fit an organization and the diverse range of people it serves. Each organization must create a program that is open to everyone, regardless of the type and severity of their disabilities. The program must cover all the geographic locations that are served by the organization. It may take time to have a program that effectively reaches everyone, and this goal must be part of the program from the start. This goal must be pursued until it is ultimately reached.

This may sound like a daunting challenge; however, it is obtainable. The good news is that it's not necessary to create each self-employment program from scratch. There are many ways to learn from the past experience of existing self-employment programs and the professional people who were involved in their creation and development. There are existing successful entrepreneurship programs whose leaders provide significant input and recommendations from their experiences with their own programs. Also, one can tap professional consultants who bring experience, innovation, direction, and leadership to the design, development, and implementation phases of the entrepreneurship program. *(See the Resource Listing in the Appendix.)* Finally, there already exist definable components for entrepreneurship programs for people with disabilities as outlined in this book that can serve as the framework for the design of the program.

Entrepreneurship Program Components for People with Disabilities

The primary components for an entrepreneurship programs for persons with disabilities are:

Orientation for Prospective Entrepreneurs

The self-employment program is explained to prospective participants, describing what the program offers and what is required of them. Participants gain a realistic perspective of the business world (see box at right) and learn the types and level of support that they will receive from the organization. Support begun in the orientation process is consistent and ongoing, continuing through training, business planning, and development of the business.

Selection Process for Entrepreneurs with a Disability

The best method of selection is self-assessment by the prospective entrepreneur. A prospective entrepreneur is given the opportunity to develop and evaluate the feasibility of a small business concept. He or she will receive support, guidance, and training to optimize the probability of developing this business concept successfully. The prospective entrepreneur has the option of returning to conventional employment at any time during this development phase, if he or she does not find self-employment an appropriate long-term employment choice.

Entrepreneurship Education and Training

Training must be both physically and cognitively accessible for persons with disabilities. Entrepreneurial education for people with disabilities may include classroom instruction, coaching as an adjunct training method either in or outside of the classroom, or one-on-one business training and coaching.

A Perspective on Business Start-ups

Bob Arnold, a CPA who has spent his career working with and assisting small business owners, presents this perspective on small business start-up and ownership.

- The successful owner has a compelling idea or vision.
- The successful owner has the drive to make that business vision a reality.
- The successful owner has experience or learns about the business that he or she wants to create.
- The owner should not worry about the financial needs to start a business. If the idea is compelling, then he or she should be able to find financing.
- The owner should put together a well-designed business plan, often with professional assistance.
- Organizational skills, financial skills, etc., should be hired or purchased if the owner does not have these skills or the time to do them, or if his or her time is better spent on other aspects of the business.
- Marketing and/or selling is essential but does not need to be done by the owner, and marketing needs vary with the type of business.
- Adaptability is of utmost importance. The business plan cannot predict the reality of unforeseen problems, market changes, customer actions, and many other variables. Each year of a business will have variations and unanticipated turns.
- Follow-up on a regular basis is essential to understand changes and/or problems and making needed adjustments on a timely basis.
- Rely on advisors before decisions are made or problems occur. Owners cannot do it all themselves. Rely on professional advisors and employees at a meaningful time in the decision process.
- A business can take years to be successful and may see ups and downs before success is achieved. To achieve and maintain success, the company must adapt to changes in economic conditions and to market changes affecting its product or service.

Training provides contact with other people who are actively engaged in their own businesses or are learning to be entrepreneurs. It is directed toward understanding what is required of an entrepreneur, understanding the challenges of entrepreneurship, and learning methods for successful business ownership. Part of this training involves business planning, including producing a business feasibility study or a business plan. However, the training focuses on success-oriented methods for business ownership rather than the mechanical aspect of putting together a business plan.

Entrepreneurship training provides guidance, direction, and assistance to the prospective business owners in developing a business plan. Guidance includes access to economic, industrial, and business resources both for research purposes and business development.

The program requires the prospective entrepreneur to work energetically and pro-actively to create a potentially successful plan for his or her business.

Personal Commitment by the Entrepreneur with Disabilities

Commitment in considerable personal time, effort and energy by the prospective businessperson is a strong component of success. The prospective entrepreneur needs to develop a personal level of comfort with the concepts underlying his or her business in order to maintain a positive and confident attitude. Commitment and participation by family or household members provide significant support, expertise, and stability.

Education and Training in Skills for the Selected Business

People with disabilities receive the same or comparable skill-related training for self-employment as for conventional employment.

Financial Assistance for the Business

Entrepreneurs with disabilities often need financial assistance to purchase accommodative technology or to make modifications to workspace to be on a more equal footing with non-disabled entrepreneurs. They may need financial assistance for any aspect of their business start-up, including capital equipment, furniture, rent deposit, and initial working capital for all aspects of the business.

Funding can come from a range of organizations involved in human services, economic development, and small business development. Loans may be obtained from the micro-loan funds that support small business development. The entrepreneur with disabilities who has gone through small business training and has developed a feasible business plan becomes a better qualified candidate from a micro-loan program.

Financial Commitment by the Entrepreneur with Disabilities

Whenever possible, entrepreneurs with disabilities participate in financing the business start-up. This financial participation can come either from their own financial resources or from a business loan. When business owners invest financially in their own businesses, their level of commitment and likelihood of success increases. Paying off loans is an additional incentive for the entrepreneur to stay with the business during hard times.

Natural Support Systems

Natural supports for the business owner go beyond the scope of the business. Some of the people who function as natural business supports also provide stability, structure, insight, and emotional support on a personal basis. These supports include, but are not limited to, business partners, family and household members, employees, subcontractors, vendors, business associates, mentors, business consultants, government agencies, nonprofit organizations, CPAs, and lawyers. Nonprofit and government organizations that provide personal services, products, and support give the entrepreneur a stronger opportunity for business success.

Partnerships

Partnerships bring businesspeople together to increase the likelihood of success for their businesses. Formal and informal partnerships always should be considered when creating a small business venture to bring new and different skills, creativity, support and energy, and additional financial resources into the business.

Support for the Business after Start-Up

A quality self-employment program provides professional referrals and business consulting while the business is developing. This assistance from professionals such as business consultants, CPAs, and lawyers continues after the business is running. Professional services may be subsidized by the entrepreneurship program for a period of time after start-up. A self-employment program also provides the entrepreneur with support in measuring and evaluating the progress of the business against the goals and milestones in the business plan.

Mentorship programs are an adjunct to the entrepreneurship program. These are volunteer programs in which active or retired businesspeople provide guidance and support for entrepreneurs with disabilities. Mentors are often in similar or related businesses. Mentors with disabilities can assist the new entrepreneurs in finding ways to be competitive with non-disabled business owners.

The Role of Small Human Services Organizations

Small human services organizations may not be able to create or support all of the needed program components. However, these organizations can collaborate with other agencies to provide a full range of services. Such collaboration is an essential aspect of success in providing opportunities for self-employment for people with disabilities.

This collaboration is not limited to organizations that include people with disabilities in their mission. Collaborative partners include economic development organizations at the state, county, or city level; job development programs, community businesses; small business loan funds; self-employment training programs; SBA resources; and entrepreneur programs at community colleges.

Integrating Components of the Entrepreneurship Program

Although there are definable components for a self-employment program, these components are not discrete steps in a set sequence. On the contrary, these components overlap. A prospective entrepreneur likely will move back and forth through these components on the way to developing a business.

Frequently Asked Questions

The following questions are frequently asked by human services counselors who have people interested in pursuing self-employment:

Q. When an individual approaches me about self-employment, how do I say "yes" and have confidence that he or she will succeed? Conversely, how do I say "no" in way that he or she will accept the decision?
A. When a program supports an individual to learn, develop skills, and assess his or her own business concept, it is the individual who ultimately will make the decision. The human services counselor gives the person access to professional business training and consulting, where there will be realistic evaluations of the business plan and the prospective entrepreneur.

Q. Can I predict if a business will fail, even when the business plan looks good?
A. There are no guarantees that any employment option will succeed, whether it is a conventional job or self-employment. However, there is increased likelihood that the business will succeed, the more:
- personally active the prospective entrepreneur is in planning
- focused and well-defined the business concept
- contact he or she has with people in the business world
- he or she understands and addresses business and disability challenges

144

- he or she has contact with potential or active customers
- he or she tests the business on a small scale

Q. Can the hard work and stress of the business cause the person's disabilities to increase, or cause relapses to conditions that are in remission or under control?
A. The person with the disabilities must understand emotionally as well as intellectually what he or she is getting into as a business owner. If physical, cognitive, or mental health problems could increase, the person with disabilities should plan in advance how to mitigate this situation through:
- determining adequate accommodations to minimize adverse health effects
- determining methods for maintaining health in conjunction with health professionals
- networking with other small business owners to help deal with stress and uncertainty
- creating support systems for physical and emotional aspects of the disabilities
- creating time and methods for relaxation and separation from the business
- defining, and possibly putting limitations on, the scope of the business
- defining, and possibly putting limitations on, his or her role in the business

Q. Is it fair to require entrepreneurs with disabilities to use loans as part of the financing for their businesses?
A. It is not only fair to have entrepreneurs with disabilities use loans for their businesses, but it is often a positive step toward long-term success. The small business owners who obtain business loans normally guarantee them both through the business and personally. This action shows a much stronger commitment to the business than when prospective entrepreneurs are given financing without a requirement to repay the funds. Simply, people who personally guarantee their loan are motivated to make the business succeed in order to pay off their debts.

Also, having a business loan makes the entrepreneur more conscious of the cash flow needs of the business. Micro-loan and conventional lenders require regular business financial reporting, which is a positive step to understanding and managing the business.

Micro-loan organizations often provide business training and assistance to the businesses who borrow from them. If a loan is obtained when the business first starts up and it is paid back in a timely manner, the business owner will have a loan history and a relationship with a financial organization. This greatly will enhance the chances of obtaining a new loan if money is required as the business grows or if there are temporary cash flow needs. Even micro-loans for a few hundred dollars can serve these purposes.

Q. How much money should our organization, or other collaborative groups, give or loan to start a business for a person with disabilities?
A. Although there is no set figure, many businesses can be started for under $5,000. However, each situation must be individually assessed to optimize success for the business. Under-funding a business destines it to failure. Keeping the business focused on a single, obtainable goal often helps to keep start-up costs down. This strategy also makes it simpler for the new owner to learn how to run the business, while decreasing the odds of making costly mistakes.

Q. When should our organization stop providing money to the business? If the business owner with disabilities asks for more money, should our organization give more money to keep the business running?
A. If money is given outright it should be provided primarily as part of the business start-up. After the business is established and stable, the entrepreneur with disabilities usually is responsible for additional financing. This is normally done by reinvesting profits into the business or by obtaining a business loan. With the exception of micro-loans, these business loans usually will require both business and personal collateral. Finding investors is another means to bring financing into a growing business.

If money is given or loaned to a business after start-up, it should be to support a successful enterprise, not to save a failing one. Money often is not the solution to a problem. Throwing money into a business may cover up problems rather than resolving them.

Q. What information should be in the financial section of the business plan?
A. Financial plans usually include:
- Balance Sheet for the business, if there are any assets or debts
- Net Worth Statement for the individual(s) starting the business
- Financial Plan for the personal expenses of the individual(s)
- Profit and Loss Statement for existing businesses, with revenues and expenses (by category) for the last one to three years
- Estimated Profit and Loss Statement, with revenues and expenses (by category) projected monthly for the next twelve months. (Estimated Profit and Loss Statement Projections beyond the next twelve months are difficult and tenuous, particularly for a new business. You should do these only if they can be based on realistic assumptions, or if they are required by a financial institution.)
- Anticipated Capital Expenditures for the next year, and further into the future if there is a reasonable basis for the projections
- Financial Assistance Plan, outlining the business' financial require-

ments and its needs for financial assistance. It should include likely resources for financial assistance and the business owner's anticipated scheduling for repaying any loans

Q. As a human services counselor, what should my role be for an individual who wishes to pursue self-employment?
A. The precise role of the counselor varies, depending on the mission and goals of the organization, the knowledge and experience of the counselor, the amount of time available, and the needs of the consumers. However, most counselors will work in a collaborative manner to guide and support an individual through the self-employment program, providing him or her access to training programs, business consultants, and other resources that are needed to develop a successful business. A crucial role of the counselor is to balance compassion for the person's self-employment goals with the realities of the business world.

Q. How do I know if I am giving the individual the correct, or adequate, training and resources?
A. Rather than making the business plan the sole focus of the planning process, balance that focus with what the person needs to succeed as an entrepreneur with disabilities, including dealing with support needs from disabilities that affect the competitiveness of the business.

Q. How do I provide all of the necessary services for the individuals I serve?
A. Collaboration with organizations that support and promote new business ventures is an essential aspect in bringing the necessary services to entrepreneurs with disabilities. The next chapter discusses the collaborative process with nonprofit and government organizations, and with businesspeople who support small business.

Source:
1. Personal communication with Robert Arnold, CPA, Roger Nittler and Co., Inc., Denver, Colorado (1999).

Chapter 10
Collaboration

Throughout this book, the theme of collaboration has underscored the processes that led to business success for all entrepreneurs, not just those with disabilities. Examples abound in the world of computer technology, electronics, and telecommunications. Many of the youthful Silicon Valley and Internet entrepreneurs brought in "adult" management teams to manage the businesses, allowing the youthful company founders to focus on developing their products and services in a time-sensitive, competitive environment. Both new and established technology companies partner or merge with other companies in the same or related fields to have expanded access to new technologies, skilled workers, and broader markets and to become more competitive entities. Collaborations, both internal and external, are also essential factors for successful self-employment programs for people with disabilities.

This is because a collaborative self-employment program makes effective use of each person's time, including human services staff members, collaborative partners, and people with disabilities. It also brings extensive outside resources to the self-employment program that could not be created within the organization due to costs, manpower needs, or lack of expertise. Finally, collaboration creates a positive working environment for both human services staff members and people with disabilities.

Where Collaboration Fits into Self-Employment Programs

Collaboration occurs within human services organizations between:
- human services organization committee members designing the self-employment program
- self-employment program trainers and human services staff members
- human services staff members throughout the organization, including those serving people with differing disabilities and in diverse locations and economic settings
- human services counselors and the people with disabilities whom they serve

Collaboration also occurs with a myriad of external resources:
1. Resources for designing, creating, and developing the self-employment program:
   - organizations and advocacy groups for people with disabilities, who support self-employment as a viable employment choice
   - state and national programs that have active and successful self-employment programs for people with disabilities
   - professionals and consultants who have experience with, and actively support, self-employment programs for people with disabilities
2. Resources to provide entrepreneurs with disabilities with a broad range of services and support for creating successful businesses. These resources include technology and support to overcome limitations from disabilities, as well as assistance in building and sustaining the business:
   - government agencies and nonprofit organizations serving people with disabilities, including assistive technology, job training, personal care services, and support services for people with disabilities and their families
   - government agencies and nonprofit organizations serving start-up or existing small businesses, including small business training, business micro-loans, and business mentorship
   - for-profit companies that provide services and products for small businesses who will work collaboratively with entrepreneurs with disabilities

Collaboration within Human Services

A superb example of a collaboration to promote self-employment for people with disabilities from the Rural Institute (University of Montana) is the Micro-Loan Fund for Entrepreneurs with Disabilities. This project lends small amounts of money to entrepreneurs with disabilities, and was funded by the US Social Security Administration and Rehabilitation Services Administration.

Initially entrepreneurs with disabilities generated business plans and incubation funds through grants via:
- Vocational Rehabilitation (nationwide, vocational rehabilitation funds about 5,000 small business start-ups annually)
- The Montana Job Training Partnership (Job Training Partnership Act/ US Department of Labor)
- Plans for Achieving Self Support (PASS) through the Social Security Administration

Unfortunately, many individuals with disabilities are not able to generate the funds necessary to launch their businesses due to their inability to qualify for credit, the limited funds and policy restrictions of the general rehabilitation system, and perceived risks to their own Social Security benefits.

EFFECTIVE TRAINING TEACHES HOW TO CREATE A SELF-EMPLOYMENT PROGRAM THAT IS OPEN TO A FULL RANGE OF PEOPLE WITH DISABILITIES WITHOUT OVERBURDENING THE WORK LOAD OF HUMAN SERVICES COUNSELORS.

To address these start-up issues, the Rural Institute and Montana Community Development Corporation (MCDC) approached the Missoula City Council. MCDC is particularly skilled at small business start-ups and generally serves nontraditional customers through their loan programs and their Small Business Development Center funded through the Small Business Administration. In this case, MCDC sought funds to cross-train various staff in business planning, loan processes, disability awareness, rehabilitation system policies, and Social Security regulations. While most of this work has been accomplished through collaborative training, money was needed to establish a "risk pool" to pay off bad debts in case an entrepreneur defaulted on a loan.

The Missoula City Council provided $10,000 to establish this safety net, thus allowing entrepreneurs with disabilities to access approximately five to twelve loans annually, ranging between $5,000 and $50,000 per year. MCDC has high-risk loan funds available for small business. The risk pool allows individuals with poor credit ratings to access the funds for business start-up and expansion.

Referrals to the loan fund come primarily from the local vocational rehabilitation office, although the Montana Job Training Partnership, the Rural Institute, and other service providers may also make application. The general flow of the loan process will be:

- referral to the Rural Institute by vocational rehabilitation to consult on the business idea and to investigate the use of Social Security Work Incentives, such as PASS
- referral on to MCDC for feasibility, business plan refinement, and market demand research
- possible loan guarantee sign-off by the local vocational rehabilitation office
- final loan package design and submission for funding

This pilot project led to submission of a foundation grant to expand the loan program into several rural communities across Montana. Currently there are several entrepreneurs developing their ideas and business plans. And perhaps the most exciting aspect of this loan fund is that it is replicable in most communities across the US, with only a minor amount of money needed to access existing loan funds.

SOME ENTREPRENEURS WITH DISABILITIES HAD SUCCESSFUL BUSINESSES BEFORE CONTACTING HUMAN SERVICES AGENCIES FOR ASSISTANCE. THESE PEOPLE ARE EXCELLENT RESOURCES TO LEARN ABOUT THE WORKINGS AND NEEDS OF SMALL BUSINESS OWNERS WITH DISABILITIES.

Training

Chapter 9 demonstrates the importance of collaboration in the design of the self-employment program. That collaboration continues in the training of human services staff members, including both counselors and support staff. This process ensures that employees throughout the organization have the opportunity to understand the self-employment program's benefits and requirements for the people being served.

Effective training demonstrates how a self-employment program works from start to finish for both human services staff and for people with disabilities. It shows how to effectively work with people who wish to pursue self-employment and how the program serves the needs of the organization's diverse customers, including those with different types and severity of disabilities and those who live in urban vs. rural locations.

Training shows how each staff member can best contribute to the self-employment program and how to effectively find and share self-employment resources with other staff members. Good training teaches how to create a self-employment program that is open to a full range of people with disabilities without overburdening the work load of human services counselors.

Staff Members

Collaboration among staff members means that each counselor does not need to start from scratch finding resources for the people with disabilities seeking self-employment. However, it does take time to develop and implement a means for sharing information. Since human services workers often have heavy work loads, it is not likely that a system will evolve unless there is an affirmative effort to create it. The system may be as simple as sending out a broadcast e-mail message when a good resource is located. Or it may be more elaborate, such as creating a database that can be searched by category, e.g., type of resource, location, and type of disability.

Whatever system you decide upon, it must be realistic in terms of:
- the time and money needed to develop it.
- ease of use by counselors and people served
- providing meaningful and accurate information
- methods for maintaining the system to ensure its usefulness over time

SELF-EMPLOYMENT PROGRAMS FOR PEOPLE WITH DISABILITIES SHOULD COLLABORATE WITH GOVERNMENT AND NONPROFIT ORGANIZATIONS THAT SUPPORT SMALL BUSINESSES.

People with Disabilities

Counselors who work collaboratively with people with disabilities are creating a positive, supportive environment in which individuals will have the confidence to learn, grow personally, gain self-esteem, make well-thought-out decisions, and take calculated risks. These are all fundamental skills for a prospective business owner.

Abraham Maslow's work from the 1950s and 1960s is currently being rediscovered by the business and academic communities. His views on effective methods of working with employees readily can be applied to the working interactions of human services counselors and prospective entrepreneurs with disabilities. Maslow insists that employment should give the worker the opportunity to go beyond physiological and safety needs, providing the opportunity to reach higher goals regarding personal relationships, learning, succeeding, and self-esteem.[1] Self-employment very clearly provides opportunities for growth and improvement for people with disabilities seeking a challenging environment.

When human services counselors work collaboratively with persons with disabilities to provide support, confidence, education, and growth, they are going a long way toward enhancing peoples' chances of becoming successful entrepreneurs. Including business partners and supportive family members or life partners in this process is part of a collaborative effort.

Additionally, human services counselors can learn from prospective entrepreneurs with disabilities. One reason that many counselors feel uncomfortable working with people with disabilities who are interested in self-employment is that counselors have had little professional exposure to small business ownership and management.

Each individual with a disability who plans and develops a business provides the counselor with an opportunity to learn about entrepreneurship and the resources available for people interested in starting their own businesses. Some entrepreneurs with disabilities had successful businesses before contacting human services agencies for assistance. These experienced entrepreneurs are excellent resources to human services counselors in understanding the workings and needs of small business owners with disabilities.

Collaboration with External Resources

The previous chapter addressed the importance of collaborative efforts and professional guidance in designing a self-employment program. The relationships developed during the design phase should continue as the program develops over time.

A new self-employment program doubtlessly will have unexpected situations that need to be dealt with constructively. Additionally, the program should evolve and expand over time. The people who helped with the initial design of the self-employment program will become knowledgeable about the organization's program as well as self-employment program strategies in general. They should remain allies in the development and growth of the organization's self-employment program for people with disabilities.

Government Agencies and Nonprofit
Organizations Serving People with Disabilities

Many of these organizations provide assistance for conventional employment for people with disabilities. However, they may not understand how the needs of entrepreneurs with disabilities differ from those of people in conventional employment. Educating these organizations about the needs of self-employed persons with disabilities can open the door to collaboration. The needs of self-employed people are varied, from assistive technology to

---

Financial Support of Entrepreneurs with Disabilities

There are business and economic development organizations throughout the country which provide access to micro-loans for people who cannot qualify for conventional business loans. David Wohl, from the Cincinnati Development Fund, addresses the diversity of these loan programs:

"...There are peer support models, training-based models, models based on fairly traditional credit analysis but adapted to the needs of very small and underserved borrowers, etc. Let a thousand flowers bloom!"[2]

Human services organizations can create alliances with micro-loan programs, which will enhance a person's chances of obtaining loans for the business. Human services organizations also can work more pro-actively in assisting with financing businesses through one or more of the following:

- providing direct financial support for the start-up business
- providing equity to the business as part of the financial package to help obtain a business loan
- assisting the business in obtaining investment capital
- obtaining economic/community development funding/loans
- providing a loss reserve fund to guarantee business loans with existing financial institutions
- creating a micro-loan program for entrepreneurs with disabilities
- providing funds to an existing micro-loan program, for specific use by entrepreneurs with disabilities

---

personal services, to healthcare and emotional support. When an organization understands the role that it can play in assisting in self-employment for people with disabilities, it can become an integral part of the self-employment program.

Government Agencies and Nonprofit
Organizations Serving Small Businesses

There are a myriad of government and nonprofit organizations supporting small businesses that are either starting up or are growing. Self-employment programs for people with disabilities should collaborate with these organizations to create optimal opportunities for prospective entrepreneurs with disabilities. In some cities and states, many of these organizations work together in a network that provides a wide range of services, including small business training and business plan development, business advice and consulting before start-up, small business loans to companies that cannot obtain or afford conventional business loans, and business guidance and mentorship after the business start-up. Self-employment programs for people with disabilities can contribute to these networks, as well as benefitting from them, by providing services to other organizations' participants who have disabilities.

There are collaborative challenges to bringing in business and economic development organizations to work with prospective entrepreneurs with disabilities. The organizations need to be informed regarding challenges to entrepreneurs with disabilities, including:

- business hurdles specific to entrepreneurs with disabilities
- obvious and hidden business costs for people with disabilities, and methods to forestall or eliminate the losses
- difficulty qualifying for minority-focused financial resources
- potential loss of government benefits specific to people with disabilities
- use of PASS and other SSA work incentives to help fund and support small businesses owned by people with disabilities
- issues related to multiple disabilities and business ownership[3]

They also need to understand what the available resources are specifically for entrepreneurs with disabilities. This list includes state vocational rehabilitation services, Social Security Administration work incentives, and nonprofit organizations whose mission is to provide assistance for people with disabilities. In addition, there is assistive technology and how to obtain it at the least cost through rehabilitation programs, grants, or loans; Veterans Administration programs for veterans with disabilities pursuing self-employment; and social service, family, and community resources.[4]

Taking the time and making the effort to communicate with business and economic development organizations will create a strong program for entrepreneurs with disabilities. It will allow the organization to be part of a larger effort to bring self-employment, and the opportunity for self-sufficiency, to a wide range of people who are socially or economically deprived.

For-Profit Companies That Provide Services and Products for Small Businesses

For entrepreneurs with disabilities to succeed, they need to actively be a part of the business world. Consequently, they need to work with numerous for-profit companies who can provide the goods and services that are necessary for the entrepreneurs to run their businesses successfully. A significant role for a self-employment program is to find for-profit companies that focus on small business customers and provide goods and services at reasonable prices, while providing high quality customer support. Some of these vendors will sell goods or services to the newly established business on an ongoing basis, becoming a critical part of how the new enterprise works in the future.

Vendor companies interested in being associated with a self-employment program can be educated though training and experience to understand the needs of entrepreneurs with disabilities. Entrepreneurs with disabilities who have existing businesses should be recruited actively as part of this vendor program. These entrepreneurs understand the challenges of doing business when the owner has disabilities. In turn, the program creates a greater market for existing businesses owned by people with disabilities.

This type of interaction brings human services and the business community together in a manner where all benefit. The self-employment program provides sound business resources for the people it serves, and entrepreneurs with disabilities have effective vendors to help build their emerging businesses. Also, vendors with or without disabilities have a "niche market" for their products and services.

Understanding Is Necessary for Collaborative Success

In order for collaboration to succeed, the participants involved must understand the successful strategies for business planning and business ownership for people with disabilities. They must debunk the myths about the limitation of people with disabilities, particularly in regard to self-employment.

All parties must utilize the owner-oriented approach to business planning for people with disabilities, which emphasizes the capabilities and needs of the business owner. This approach views disabilities as challenges that can be overcome rather than roadblocks to success.

Participants should explore the extensive methods that a business owner with disabilities can use to create accommodations, partnerships, and business relations that lead to a successful business venture. They must employ creative thinking and problem-solving methods for business planning that will give the entrepreneur tools for dealing with the challenges and changes in the marketplace and the economy, as well as with challenges and changes in his or her disabilities. This common basis of understanding will facilitate the collaborative efforts of the self-employment program, its human services, business, and economic development partners, and the people with disabilities who seek self-employment as their means for employment and economic growth.

Sources:
1. Maslow, Dr. Abraham H., (1998). *Maslow on Management*, New York: John Wiley and Sons, Inc.
2. Wohl, David, (1999). Posting, Cincinnati Development Fund, Community Development e-mail listserv.
3. Weiss-Doyel, Alice. (May 1997), "Vocational Rehabilitation: Opportunity for Collaboration," AEO Annual Conference.
4. Ibid.

Self-Employment for People with Severe Disabilities:
An Interview with David Hammis

David Hammis works extensively with people with severe developmental and psychiatric disabilities in their pursuit of conventional employment and self-employment, and with the organizations that are designed to assist and support people with severe disabilities. Hammis is personally responsible for the implementation of over 150 Plans for Achieving Self Support (PASS). He has developed over 175 jobs for individuals with severe and multiple disabilities. Hammis managed and provided the training and technical assistance for the Wyoming Supported Employment Systems Change Project, which substantially increased the use of Social Security Work Incentives in Wyoming, producing eighty-eight new PASSs statewide in three years. In Oregon, Hammis provided Vocational Rehabilitation Work Incentive Specialist training, in conjunction with the Eugene, Oregon, Small Business Administration and Microsoft Corporation. The training developed ten small businesses based on peer-written work-incentive support, yielding over 400 PASSs in three years in Oregon. In Ohio, Hammis has provided ongoing work incentive and career planning support for the Ohio Conversion Project for over four years. Graduates of his Work Incentives Benefits training programs have developed hundreds of PASSs and applications for Social Security Work Incentives. Hammis received the International Association for Persons in Supported Employment Professional of the Year award in 1996. He worked at the Rural Institute (University of Montana) as the Montana Consumer Controlled Careers (MC3) project director, training coordinator for the Research in Social Security Employment Supports (RISES) Project, an organizational consultant, disability benefits specialist, and rehabilitation/employment engineer. In 2000, Hammis opened a human services consulting firm in partnership with Cary Griffin with self-employment as one of their areas of expertise.

What is the typical amount of time it takes for entrepreneurs with severe disabilities to (1) create a viable business concept, (2) research the business concept and do the business planning, (3) get the business established (not necessarily profitable)?

There really is no magic number, and the variation is quite wide and individualized. However, I would like to dispel the myth that business plans and small business development require years to develop. I believe that most people can accomplish the research for the business concept, do the business planning, and get the business established in three to six months. I would note that also has been my experience for people without disabilities. I've assisted in developing a business literally overnight and one that took the better part of two years to start.

Refining the business concept and successful business planning is a slightly different matter. I would say that the time period of twelve to twenty months often produces much higher quality business, marketing, and operations plans than is found in the early development of the business.

What are the types of business challenges that tend to occur for entrepreneurs with severe disabilities?

The most common business challenges and problems that I've experienced while supporting people with substantial disabilities in business development have been associated with the multitude of human services agencies that interact with each person's life. There are many areas these organizations impact: home, healthcare, government benefits, vocational rehabilitation, and small business development. People with disabilities face the daunting challenge daily of interacting with dozens of government programs that have varying levels of controls and intrusiveness into their daily lives and decisions.

The most related business development issue is the lack of skilled business support professionals versed in the rules and regulations of relevant human services programs as well as their parallel in government small business assistance programs. This issue often results in one government agency or program creating what appears to be a stand-alone small business solution (under its program rules) for a business challenge. Yet this same solution turns into a barrier to small business development from another interrelated government program.

People become frustrated in finding that their successful closure of a business negotiation for a profitable sale of products or services is quickly and apparently attacked by multiple government programs. In such a situation, a small business owner should be celebrating, happy, enjoying life, and excited. Yet, often the lesson is not to be happy because one of the many systems she or he interacts with daily will quickly intervene to create a problem.

Here is an example to this feeling of frustration that I just described. A business owner without a disability closes a major sale and is elated. Yet this business owner knows that the IRS could easily take a substantial share of her or his profits if he or she does not fully understand the rules of the IRS system. However, if the business owner has a good accountant and learns the IRS rules and opportunities, then the cause for such concern is diminished to the manageable task of complying with the IRS rules with the help of a professional. Multiply that one concern about a government system by ten or twenty competing entities. The result is that government organizations could, as Maslow put it, impact your basic survival needs by:

- increasing your Section 8 housing rent
- reducing or taking your Social Security check
- eliminating your food stamps
- charging you up to 1000% more for your healthcare or taking it away completely
- eliminating your personal care assistance needed to simply survive each day
- in general, sending you the message that financial success is punished by government systems

There are solutions to all of these issues. However, the real issue is the paucity of consultants trained in understanding and finding equitable and profitable business solutions that fit in with the multitude of government programs surrounding people with disabilities.

I have witnessed people with disabilities in true entrepreneurial spirit move forward without having the time, for example, to find a skilled government and disability benefits consultant. They often must work through a variety of problems on their own. One individual received an unexpected SSI overpayment. Another got a letter from Medicaid that said her Medicaid was terminated, when it should not have been. Still another person was forced to move out of a small, yet comfortable apartment because the US Department of Housing and Urban Development Section 8 rules did not allow operating a home-based information technology business in government subsidized apartments.

Despite these challenges, in each case the individual has prevailed and is still in business! The best solutions have and continue to be skilled staff and consultants who know the rules of each interacting government program. Professionals must develop proactive solutions to the challenges presented by such systems to small business owners with disabilities. They then must integrate these solutions into business planning and long-term implementation and support processes for the business.

What support is necessary for entrepreneurs with severe disabilities to succeed in business?

The types of support from family, employment staff, nonemployment staff, business community members, and general community members have varied across a wide range. Without a doubt, for every operating small business I've been involved with, the key type of support for someone with a severe disability provided by one or some or all of the above groups was that *at least one person chose to believe in the person and the business idea and provided support and encouragement!*

A significant number of potential business owners with disabilities are currently waiting or demonstrating in a variety of ways their desire to start their own business. However, they are not in business due to the lack of support from people paid to serve them. This is mainly due to unfounded personal and social beliefs about people with severe disabilities being incapable of owning and operating a small business.

A comparison can be made to our service history in Montana, where not long ago 1,500 people with developmental disabilities lived in state institutions specifically for people with developmental disabilities. It was not believed that people with such disability labels could live and work in the community. But those beliefs were incorrect. As the support staff and government programs learned their beliefs were wrong, changes began to occur and community living and working supports were developed. Now our two Montana state institutions are being reviewed for complete closure, with a total of less than one hundred people still in our two institutions.

Starting a small business is almost guaranteed *not* to be an option if the family, friends, and paid support staff providing services to the individual do not support the business idea. Individuals with severe disabilities who have started and are operating businesses have either family or friends or human services staff who believe in them and support their businesses. It is one of the key components for most of the people I have had the privilege to work with over the years. Once people believe in the person's desire, social right, and capacity to own and operate a business, the next steps and levels of support develop naturally. These follow typical standard business practices and supports, with the addition of supports in navigating barriers presented in the myriad of government agencies involved in people's lives.

Appendices

Consulting Services for Self-Employment for People with Disabilities

BOLD Consulting Group
(Businesspeople Overcoming Limitations from Disabilities)

BOLD works with nonprofit and government organizations to create, expand, and provide training for entrepreneurship programs for people with disabilities. BOLD consults on all aspects of self-employment programs: candidate selection procedures, training programs in entrepreneurial skills and management, training in business planning, finding and creating loan funds for start-up and growing businesses, creating mentorship programs for ongoing businesses, and creating collaborative programs with other organizations. BOLD believes that successful business planning for people with disabilities focuses on:

1. the longevity of the business, not just its start-up
2. the quality of life of the business owner, not just his or her income
3. developing entrepreneurial skills and methods, beyond the creation of a business plan
4. understanding and overcoming the business challenges posed by disabilities
5. expanding the use and effectiveness of workplace accommodations to promote the success of the entire business

For more information on the BOLD Consulting Group, contact:

Alice Weiss Doyel
BOLD Consulting Group
Effective Compensation, Incorporated
12136 W. Bayaud Ave., Ste. 100
Lakewood, CO 80228-2115
877.RING.ECI (877-746-4324)
adoyel@effectivecompensation.com
www.effectivecompensation.com/bold-owners

Griffin - Hammis Associates, LLC

Griffin - Hammis Associates, LLC (GHA) is a full-service consultancy specializing in developing communities of economic cooperation. GHA addresses this mission by providing high-quality training and technical consultation, project development and management services, strategic planning and critical meeting facilitation, materials development, and inventive service delivery. GHA specializes in community rehabilitation improvement, job creation and job site training, employer development, Social Security benefits analysis and work incentives, self-employment feasibility and refinement, management-leadership mentoring, and civic entrepreneurship. Customers are wide-ranging and include businesses, community rehabilitation programs, state and local governments, universities, individuals, and others from the public and private sectors.

For more information on Griffin-Hammis Associates, contact:

Cary Griffin, Senior Partner	David Hammis, Senior Partner
Griffin-Hammis Associates, LLC	Griffin-Hammis Associates, LLC
5582 Klements Ln.	317 Franklin St.
Florence, MT 59833	Middletown, OH 45042
406-273-9181	513-424-6198
cgriffin@selway.umt.edu	dhammis@selway.umt.edu

www.griffinhammis.com

Enterprise Support Center

Dennis Rizzo is the founder of Enterprise Support Center, a consulting firm specializing in program creation and training in entrepreneurship for people with disabilities. Rizzo managed the merger of the former New Jersey Disability Loan Fund, Inc., and the New Jersey Community Loan Fund. Previously, he developed and ran the Disability Loan Fund from within the New Jersey Developmental Disabilities Council, from its inception in 1992.

For more information on the Enterprise Support Center, contact:

Dennis Rizzo
Enterprise Support Center
PO Box 181
Mount Holly, NJ 08060
609-702-5781
DCRiz@aol.com

Disabled Businesspersons Association

Founded in 1985 by successful business owners with disabilities, the Disabled Businesspersons Association (DBA), a charitable, all-volunteer, nonprofit membership organization, provides free self-employment/business information and assistance to enterprising individuals with disabilities and for professionals in vocational rehabilitation, career, and business counseling worldwide.

Receiving thousands of inquiries and requests for services yearly, and having assisted more than 12,000 in business, the DBA is recognized as the nation's largest and leading authority on the self-employment of people with disabilities.

For more information on the Disabled Businesspersons Association, contact:

Disabled Businesspersons Association
San Diego State University/Interwork Institute
5850 Hardy Ave., Ste. 112
San Diego, CA 92182-5313
619-594-8805
dbanet@ix.netcom.com
www.web-link.com/dba/dba.htm

Rural Institute (University of Montana)

The Rural Institute Training Department does consulting in all aspects of competitive, supported, and self-employment. The Rural Institute staff specializing in employment are especially skilled in job development, design of on-the-job training, funding, business planning, Social Security work incentives, job coaching, assessment, and operations management.

The Rural Institute Training Department staff are regular presenters of training seminars across the US and in other countries. They serve as keynote speakers at state and national conferences, and they perform on-site services to community rehabilitation agencies and state systems on a contract basis.

For more information on the Rural Institute, contact:
Cary Griffin
Rural Institute
52 Corbin Hall
The University of Montana
Missoula, MT 59812
406-243-2454
cgriffin@selway.umt.edu
www.ruralinstitute.umt.edu

Internet Resources for Self-Employment for People with Disabilities

1. BOLD Consulting Project
(Businesspeople Overcoming Limitations from Disabilities)
www.effectivecompensation.com/bold-owners
E-mail: adoyel@effectivecompensation.com

2. Montana University Affiliated Rural Institute on Disabilities
ruralinstitute.umt.edu/rtcrural/selem/ruselfem.htm
E-mail: cgriffin@selway.umt.edu

3. Disabled Businesspersons Association
www.web-link.com/dba/dba.htm
E-mail: dbanet@ix.netcom.com

4. Rehabilitation Research and Training Center on Supported Employment
Virginia Commonwealth University
www.worksupport.com/topics/entrepr2.asp

5. Diversity World.Com
"enriching workplaces and reducing employment barriers"
www.diversityworld.com, then click on "disability" and page down to self-employment/entrepreneurship
E-mail: info@diversityworld.com

Internet Resources for Business Development

There are two premiere Internet web-sites that can be used as portals to information on small business planning. These high-quality sites provide sound, basic business information and business tools. They also link to further sites and other resources on small business start-up and management.

These web sites are not directed toward entrepreneurs with disabilities, and caution should be taken not to use the information in a manner that would eliminate people with disabilities from small business ownership or put unnecessary hurdles in the path to self-employment.

1. American Express has one of the best sites for small business information. Unfortunately, the exact web address for this information changes over time. At this time, the address is: www.americanexpress.com/homepage/ smallbusiness.shtml. If the address has changed, you can go to the American Express home page at www.americanexpress.com; select the Site Directory; page down through the Site Directory until you find American Express Small Business Exchange, and click to enter. Another alternative to access this site is through a search engine, using the term American Express Small Business.

Within the American Express Small Business Exchange is the Small Business Start-Up Guide with information on these topics:
- How do I come up with a winning business idea?
- How do I research my business idea to determine if it is viable?
- Do I need to register my business?
- How do I determine what licenses and permits I will need?
- How do I get a tax ID number?
- How do I name my business? How do I protect that name?
- Should I incorporate? What other business structure options do I have?
- How much personal savings should I have before I start a business?
- Where should I look for financing?
- Do I need a business plan?

In addition, there are sections on Creating an Effective Business Plan, Common Start-up Mistakes, and Business Tools Useful to a Prospective Entrepreneur.

2. Commerce Clearing House (CCH) has a web-site called the Business Owner's Toolkit at: www.toolkit.cch.com. Within this site is an on-line business planning book, The SOHO Guidebook, containing the following chapters:
- Starting Your Business
- Planning Your Business
- Getting Financing for Your Business
- Marketing Your Product
- Your Office and Equipment
- People Who Work for You
- Managing Your Business Finances
- Controlling Your Taxes
- Building Your Personal Wealth
- Getting Out of Your Business

Additionally, CCH has an array of business tools:
- Model Business Documents: Sample letters, contracts, forms, and policies ready to be customized, including a Sample Independent Contractor Agreement and a Job Application Form.
- Financial Spreadsheet Templates: Help for managing business finances from balancing a checkbook to creating financial statements.
- Checklists: Information on whether you qualify for the home office write-off to the right things to do and say during an employee termination interview.

Internet Resources for Assistive Technology

These web-sites also have connections to other sites with further information on assistive technology.

1. The web-site of the Alliance for Technology Access (ATA) is at www.ataccess.org. The ATA is comprised of a broad network providing information and support services to children and adults with disabilities and increasing their use of standard, assistive, and information technologies. These ATA members can be found all across the country. The ATA mission is to connect children and adults with disabilities to technology tools.

ATA's on-line directory includes:
- ATA resource centers
- ATA vendor members (over eighty developers and distributors of assistive devices and software and a description of their product lines)
- ATA affiliates (a network of affiliated organizations, including other technology, disability, and assistive technology organizations)
- ATA associates (a network of individuals such as family members, advocates, and practitioners in related fields, e.g., assistive technology and occupational therapy)

The ATA on-line library provides extensive links to other assistive technology resources, methods for increasing world wide web access for people with disabilities, and an e-mail response system to questions regarding assistive technology.

2. The Assistive Technology Industry Association (ATIA) has a web-site at www.atia.org. ATIA has sixty-two full members and eleven associate members. Their on-line membership directory has links to the web-sites of almost all their members, providing full product and service information for each of the companies. Many of these company web-sites include links to other assistive technology resources. These companies' sites, taken together, provide an extensive resource in the area of assistive technology.

Recommended Books

Growing A Business
Author: Paul Hawken
Publisher: Simon and Schuster
ISBN: 0-671-67164-2
Format: Trade Paperback (US $12.00)
                Audio Cassette (US $11.00)

Paul Hawken's book is unique in providing an understanding of what it takes to nurture and grow a small business.

Business Planning Guide
Author: David Bangs
Publisher: Dearborn Trade
ISBN: 1-57410-099-8
Format: Trade Paperback (US $24.95)
                CD-Rom Book (US $34.95)

David Bangs provides the best easy-to-follow guide to creating a business plan. It is designed for use by students/novice entrepreneurs and by those persons who are more experienced in business planning.

Hoist Your Own Sails: Self-Directed
Employment for People with Disabilities
Authors: Dennis Rizzo and Elizabeth Van Houtte
Publisher: Training Resource Network, Inc.
ISBN: 1-883302-35-8
Format: Trade Paperback (US $8.00)

Dennis Rizzo and Elizabeth Van Houtte provide a clear overview of self-directed employment in an easy-to-read, twenty-six page "pocket guide." They cover direct ownership, partnerships or cooperatives, and participatory ownership such as social enterprises.

Creating Business and Corporate Initiatives for Individuals with Disabilities
Authors: Dale Verstegen and John Nietupski
Publisher: Virginia Commonwealth University
Format: Trade Paperback (US $12.95)

This guide offers hands-on strategies to develop public sector and corporate partnerships and create new jobs through integrated businesses operated by entrepreneurs with disabilities.

Government-Related Internet Resources for Business

This list focuses on a few federal government Internet web-sites as portals to government information on small business planning. These web-sites also connect you to other sites with information on small business issues.

Some of these web-sites are not directed toward entrepreneurs with disabilities, and caution should be taken not to use the information in a manner that would eliminate people with disabilities from small business ownership or put unnecessary hurdles in their path.

1. The US Small Business Administration (SBA) at www.sba.gov has extensive information regarding business start-up, on such subjects as:
- What is a Small Business?
- Your First Steps
- Do Your Research
- Training
- Business Planning
- Patents and Trademarks
- Non-Government Business Resource Links

There is an extensive on-line Small Business Start-Up Kit. Beyond the basics on business planning, the kit includes government-focused information, such as SBA loan and financial programs and how to write a loan proposal. It also covers government regulations of all aspects of business ownership and management, and offers extensive SBA Assistance Programs. In addition, it lists local resources for SBA assistance, such as SBA offices, SCORE offices, Small Business Development Centers (SBDC), Business Information Centers (BIC), Tribal BIC, and One-Stop Capital Shops.

2. SCORE, the Service Corp of Retired Executives at www.score.org has information on SCORE services, such as workshops and individual small business consulting and e-mail business consulting. The SCORE site has success stories, management tips, and their newsletter. This site has excellent connections to other web-sites for persons interested in starting and running small businesses.

3. The Job Accommodation Network (JAN) now has a Small Business and Self-Employment Service Page (SBSES) at janweb.icdi.wvu.edu/sbses. This web-site is specifically directed to people with disabilities. The SBSES is a service of the President's Committee on Employment of People with Disabili-

ties, which provides information, counseling, and referrals about self-employment and small business ownership opportunities for people with disabilities.

The SBSES can answer questions concerning starting a business and self-employment practices: from people with disabilities, human services providers, friends and family of people with disabilities, and anyone else with an interest in promoting self-employment and small business ownership as career choices for people with disabilities.

SBSES can provide information and referrals about: developing a business concept, market research, writing a business plan, obtaining capital, loan guarantees, technical assistance resources, growing a business, personnel management, financial management, developing a marketing plan, disability issues such as Social Security, PASS plans, healthcare, and working at home.

JAN's consultants have access to a database of over 200,000 accommodations to provide practical options, whether for the business owner with disabilities or for the employees, including:

- worksite modifications
- assistive technologies
- job restructuring
- modified work schedules
- other appropriate accommodations

JAN's SBSES connections to government, small business, and disability-related resources are expansive and inviting for persons who wish to research any of these subjects. SBSES information is free. There is no cost for the telephone call or for any materials. Telephone hours are Monday through Thursday from 8:00 am to 8:00 pm and Friday from 8:00 am to 7:00 pm (eastern time). Voice mail records messages after hours, weekends, and holidays at 800-526-7234 V/TT. The mailing address and fax number are:

Small Business and Self-Employment Service
Job Accommodation Network
PO Box 6080
Morgantown, WV 26506-6080
Fax: 1-304-293-5407

4.   The US Department of Labor (DOL) has a web-site at www.dol.gov. This site deals with a variety of issues that affect small businesses. Of particular interest are:

- The Small Business Compliance Assistance Information Inventory is a matrix of Department of Labor compliance assistance materials that are available on the Internet. The matrix is designed to serve as a clearinghouse for all regulatory compliance assistance documents, publications, and printed information published by DOL agencies.

- Employment Laws Assistance for Workers and Small Businesses (elaws) is an interactive system designed to help employers and employees understand and comply with numerous employment laws enforced by DOL. Each elaws advisor gives advice and provides information on a specific law or regulation based on the user's particular situation.

5. The Social Security Administration (SSA) web-site is at www.ssa.gov. This is a gargantuan site in size, complexity, and subject matter. It is recommended that you have professional assistance or infinite time and patience to fully explore this site if you are not familiar with Social Security policies.

Perhaps the easiest starting place on the Social Security Administration's web-site is at www.ssa.gov/pubs, which contains a long list of SSA publications, including a publication on Plan for Achieving Self-Support (PASS). In another area of this web-site, www.ssa.gov/online, SSA provides online access to social security forms, including the form for PASS.

Basic Social Security Definitions

The following are Social Security Administration (SSA) definitions from the SSA web-site that may assist you in understanding some of the basic SSA concepts. These are just basic definitions, and do not encompass all of the factors that you need to know to thoroughly understand these concepts.

You should verify this information with a Social Security professional advisor, since changes are made in the Social Security system on an ongoing basis. For example, the Ticket to Work and Work Incentives Improvement Act of 1999 provide improvements for people with disabilities seeking conventional employment and self-employment.

SSDI and SSI

Social Security Disability Insurance (SSDI) provides benefits to disabled or blind individuals who are "insured" by workers' contributions to the Social Security trust fund. These contributions are the Federal Insurance Contributions Act (FICA) social security taxes paid on their earnings or those of their spouses or parents.

Supplemental Security Income Program (SSI) makes cash assistance payments to aged, blind, and disabled people (including children under age eighteen) who have limited income and resources. The federal government funds SSI from general tax revenues. Some states pay benefits to some individuals to supplement their federal benefits. Some of these states have arranged with SSA to combine their supplementary payment with the federal payment into one monthly check. Other states manage their own programs and make their payments separately.

These two programs share many concepts and terms. However, there are also many very important differences in the program rules affecting eligibility and benefit payments. Some people are eligible for benefits under both programs at the same time.

Both SSDI and SSI define disability as the inability to engage in any substantial gainful activity because of a medically determinable physical or mental impairment(s) that can be expected to result in death, or that has lasted (or that can be expected to last) for a continuous period of not less than twelve months.

To be eligible for SSDI, the worker must have worked and paid Social Security taxes for enough years to be covered under Social Security insurance; some of the taxes must have been paid in recent years; and you must be:
- the worker or the worker's adult child or widow(er)
- considered medically disabled
- not working or working but earning less than the substantial gainful activity level

To be eligible for SSI based on a medical condition, you must:
- have little or no income or resources
- be a US citizen or meet the requirements for noncitizens
- be considered medically disabled;
- be a resident of the fifty states, District of Columbia, or Northern Mariana Islands

Substantial Gainful Activity

SSA evaluates the work activity of persons claiming or receiving disability benefits under SSDI, and/or claiming benefits because of a disability (other than blindness) under SSI. Under both programs, SSA uses earnings guidelines to evaluate your work activity to decide whether the work activity is substantial gainful activity and whether SSA can consider you disabled under the law. While this is only one of the tests used to decide if you are disabled, it is a critical threshold in disability evaluation.

As of 2000, if your impairment is other than blindness, earnings averaging over $700 a month generally demonstrate "substantial gainful activity." If you are blind, earnings averaging over $1,170 a month generally demonstrate substantial gainful activity.

How a Plan for Achieving Self-Support (PASS) helps SSI Recipients.

1. Who can have a PASS?

If you receive SSI or could qualify for SSI, you can have a plan. You may not need a plan now, but you may need one in the future to remain eligible or to increase your SSI payment amount.

2. What can a PASS do for you?

A PASS allows you to set aside income and/or resources for a specified time for a work goal. For example, you could set aside money for education, vocational training, or starting a business. SSA does not count the income that you set aside under your PASS when it figures your SSI payment amount. SSA also does not count the resources that you set aside under your PASS when it determines your initial and continuing eligibility for SSI.

A PASS can help you establish or maintain SSI eligibility and can increase your SSI payment amount. A PASS does not affect any substantial gainful activity determination for your initial eligibility decision.

3. What are the requirements for a PASS?

Your plan must:
- be designed especially for you
- be in writing, preferably using the SSA form: SSA-545-BK
- have a specific work goal that you are capable of performing
- have a specific time frame for reaching your goal

- show what money (other than your SSI payments) and other resources you have or receive that you will use to reach your goal
- show how your money and resources will be used to reach your work goal
- show how the money you set aside will be kept identifiable from other funds
- be approved by SSA
- be reviewed by SSA to assure your plan is actually helping you achieve progress

4. Who can help you set up a PASS?

Anyone can help you with your PASS, including vocational rehabilitation counselors, social workers, human services professionals, human services consultants, or employers. SSA evaluates the plan and decides if it acceptable. SSA also helps people put their plans in writing.

Note: It is best to use a vocational rehabilitation counselor, human services professional, or human services consultant who is *experienced and successful* in writing these plans. This is particularly important when the PASS is written for self-employment and small business start-up.

5. How does a PASS affect SSI eligibility and payment amount?

SSA does not count resources set aside under a PASS toward the resource limit. When SSA figures your SSI payment amount, it does not count income set aside under a PASS. SSA applies this exclusion to your countable income after it applies all other applicable exclusions.

6. How does **Property Essential to Self Support** (PESS) help SSI recipients?

SSA does not count some resources that are essential to your means of self-support when it decides your initial and continuing eligibility for SSI. SSA does not count property that you use in a trade or business (e.g., inventory) or use for work as an employee (e.g., tools or equipment). Other use of the items does not matter. SSA does not count up to $6,000 of equity value of nonbusiness property that you use to produce goods or services essential to daily activities (e.g., land used to produce vegetables or livestock solely for consumption by your household). SSA does not count up to $6,000 of equity value of nonbusiness income-producing property if the property yields an annual rate of return of at least 6% (e.g., rental property). However, SSA does not consider liquid resources (e.g., stock, bonds, notes) as property essential to self-support unless you use them as part of a trade or business.